I Can Learn to Pray

The Lord's Prayer

The Prayer of The Kingdom

A Christian classic of the Lord's Prayer. It is a must-read
for Christians and non-Christians alike. This book is
excellent for the Christian Community, because it serves a
dual purpose. It not only teaches one how to pray and know
God in a personal way, but it is a marvelous teaching tool
for new convert classes.

Winsome Walters

www.xulonpress.com

TABLE OF CONTENTS

IN MEMORY OF MY FATHER

Dad, thank you for the home you gave me. In your firm and steadfast way, you taught me how to live. The years go by so fast, it seems like only yesterday when you, in your own dialect and version of Solomon's proverbs, charged all of us saying – *"HEAR, ye children, the instruction of a father, and attend to know understanding. For I give you good doctrine, forsake ye not my law ... Let thine heart retain my words: keep my commandments, and live" (Proverbs 4:1-4)* ... You searched deep to find the highest thoughts and aspirations on which to hitch your life and ours.

I didn't understand you then, but now I understand you for the first time – I've become wiser *(Psalm 111:10; Proverbs 1:7)* ... I've found my way and the guide for my life ... I have given my heart to the Lord Jesus Christ. Thanks Poppa. I just want to tell you, I have found the perfect Father in heaven, and you are the closest thing to the perfect father here on earth. I may no longer need your hand for every step I take. But, I just want to tell you – I know you're still here ... Sometimes I get a glimpse of you in my own words and deeds ... I hear you speaking in my heart ... leading me on. As I head in any direction I don't know to go, I hear you calling out His name ... to show me "the Way" *(John 3:16-*

17; 14:6; 1 Timothy 2:4-6; Matthew 6:9-13 KJV). I can hear you calling out, "Child, remember the first and most important command *(Matthew 22:37-40 NLT)* ... If you love me, obey me" *(John 14:15).*

Dad ... I want you to know, the greatest gift I ever had ... is called Dad! You never stood as tall as when you knelt to pray with me. No matter how tall I've grown, you will always be someone I look up to ... and I know you're up there ... I hear you calling me to keep on keeping on.

$\mathcal{P}$

Revelation flows ... Scriptures unfold ... God
the Father's heart is revealed as you read the
pages ... You grasp God's love for all humanity.
This absolutely, fascinating and timely book
belongs in every home. Its deeply inspirational
influence makes it destined to become one of the
great personal discipleship books of our time.
It is a worthwhile text to knowing God as the
generous and loving Father of mankind, and for
understanding the true principle of the spirit of
prayer as it relates to knowing God's will and the
deepest religious yearnings of mankind seeking to
find "the Way" (*John 3:16-17; 14:6; 1 Timothy 2:4-
6; Matthew 6:9-13 KJV*).

ENDORSEMENTS

⌁

Winsome Walters writes with refreshing enthusiasm, assurance, anticipation, and hope about God's plan for our lives, and shows the loving, faithful heart of the heavenly Father. One key faith lesson lies in the realization that the earth and all creation is a fundamental gift of God, whose word creates and sustains community, and helps people become their best selves. When we are firmly anchored to the One who is the bedrock of our faith, it is comforting to know that we don't have to face life alone, that indeed we have someone related to us in a special way as the generous and loving "Father" of mankind. Without His direction we can't know where we are going. We can learn to trust God and let Him provide and position us to find strength and wisdom, and to know with certainty our ultimate destiny.

Dr. Rosalie S. Johnson
    Elected Community Leader and Former City Government Official – District of Columbia Government, Ward 6 Advisory Neighborhood Commissioner (ANC) 6A09

This book, *I Can Learn to Pray – **The Lord's Prayer** – The Prayer of The Kingdom*, is a God-ordained, Spirit-filled book that will lead you straight to the heart and will of God. Of the many writings on prayer that I have read, I have never read a book on prayer that is so captivating. It is not only a work that will hold your interest, but it will teach you how to find Christ and how to pray once you have found Him. It is a must-read for Christians and non-Christians alike. This book is excellent for the Christian Community, because it serves a dual purpose. It not only teaches one how to pray and know God in a personal way, but it is a marvelous teaching tool for new convert classes. It is sure to be considered a classic in Christian discipleship in the years to come. To God be the glory for Winsome and this wonderful, spiritual, very creative and scholarly text.

Dr. Thaddeus Steele, M.B.A., M.Div., Ph.D., CEO
Power Place, Inc., Potter's Transformation Center

A biblical and edifying personal way on how to pray the Lord's Prayer.

Rev. Joseph G. Donders, Ph.D., Author
- Charged with the Spirit: Mission is for Everyone
- Risen Life: Healing a Broken World
- Creation and Human Dynamism: A Spirituality for Life
- Non-Bourgeois Theology: An African Experience of Jesus
- Jesus, the Way: Reflections on the Gospel of Luke
- Seven Days with the Gospel of John: A Personal Retreat
- Seven Days with the Gospel of Luke
- Jesus, the Stranger: Reflections on the Gospels

Revelation flows ... Scriptures unfold ... God the Father's heart is revealed as you read the pages ... You grasp God's love for all humanity. This absolutely, fascinating and timely book belongs in every home. It gives a new and insightful perspective on how anyone can achieve a better life, and is an appealing book which can be enjoyed by adults as well as young people. Its deeply inspirational influence makes it destined to become one of the great personal discipleship books of our time.

Remigius Demby
Amen Foundation, Inc.

A Christian classic of the Lord's Prayer. It deserves a wide reading audience, and has a wonderful sense of time and place.

Jaime Vega
Rincon Cristiano de Maryland Bookstore

M y true relationship is with God to fulfill my obliga-
tions to Him. To take the measures of truth which
He has given me and propel them on to usefulness in the
Kingdom, to accomplish His plan and purpose in the world.
And it takes time and a different kind of aptitude to craft a
skill in us to wield the most potent weapon on the face of the
earth – letting the mind be in us, which was also in Christ
Jesus *(Philippians 2:5 KJV)*, aligning our will with God's
will; seeking first His Kingdom and His righteousness – to
accomplish His plan and purpose in the world to conquer
evil and set us free from sin and death, securing the present
safety and the eternal salvation of humanity through Christ
Jesus His Son, our Savior and Lord, and what He has done
for us at the cross.

Through our faith, we COME to Christ. And through our
faith in Christ Jesus we assume our responsibility to GO and
TELL the Good News saying, "This is what I've seen … this
is what I've heard … this is what I know about Christ." If we
are to know Him, we cannot just read the writings of others
who have been touched by Him. We must come to Him and
let Him teach us about Himself, so that we can know Him for
ourselves and let Him change us from within.

Winsome Walters

FOREWORD

⌐𝒫

I am honored to write a foreword for *I Can Learn to Pray – The Lord's Prayer – The Prayer of The Kingdom*. Each time I read the words, I come away refreshed. Anyone who reads this book will not only find strength and wisdom to walk life's pathway, but will certainly be encouraged to live with the enthusiasm and joy of serving God.

Someone said, "An optimist goes to the window every morning and says, 'Good morning, God.' The pessimist goes to the window and says, 'Good God! ... Morning!'" But I believe, that the difference between a "Good morning, God" and a "Good God! ... Morning!" is to let Jesus come into our hearts.

I Can Learn to Pray – The Lord's Prayer – The Prayer of The Kingdom wants everyone's outlook on life to become like that of the optimist – one of hopefulness ... because we have come to faith in God ... we have found the way *(John 14:6)* ... we have come to the place where He will bless us.

God has a Word for our generation and a will to see us triumph in this life and throughout eternity. His ultimate purpose will be fulfilled and all the families of the earth blessed when we leave our old lives behind and follow Him to the place where He will bless us *(Genesis 12:1-3 NKJV)*.

From the message in this book, we come to know that we are in God's thoughts at all times because He cares for us. That He loves and forgives us long before we ever knew Him, and everyone on earth is precious in His sight. Like Him, I encourage and invite the sinner to come to Him and the wanderer to return *(Luke 15:18)*.

This book illustrates that when we learn the truth, we will realize that we are like lost sheep gone astray, we are sinners doomed to die *(Romans 7:9)*, but that God has sent us help to find the way *(John 14:6)*, and that if we leave our old lives behind and come to Christ just as we are, wherever we are, we will find our way and the guide for our lives. Christ knows what human means – He knows we're not perfect ... and the soul that sins, it shall die *(Genesis 2:17; Ezekiel 18:4, 20-24; Romans 3:23; 5:12; 6:23)*. He comes to ensure the future for those who would let Him shape it – this is the gift that Christ has brought us *(John 3:16- 17 NIV; 17:3 NIV)*. He did not come to perform the function of "religion" but rather to fulfill God's inner spiritual intention – the law of love and grace which accepts us as we are but cares enough about us to tell us the *truth* about our real condition, and that He intends to change us and set us free from the predicament of our sinful nature This is the truth Christ brings to all mankind *(John 18:37)*. All God asks is that we **believe**.

Christ is the messenger of love, the fountain of life, and the mystery of God's grace. He is the One in tune with the diverse challenges and joys of our lives. When we come to Him for the gift He has brought us, we have come to the place where we will be blessed.

The reality that God cares so much to send us such a sacrificial gift *(John 3:16-17 NIV; 17:3 NIV)* is the thing that gives life its deepest significance.

Rev. Jose R. Arce
Casa del Alferero Asambleas De Dios

INTRODUCTION

⌒

There is one lesson that all should learn – that it is absolutely necessary to fellowship with God each day and to know Him as the generous and loving Father of mankind. The father-child relationship between God and man is brought about through prayer. Christ has given His disciples a sample of the true principle of spiritual prayer. Through the Lord's Prayer we have access to the Father. The Lord's Prayer opens the way for God's awesome truths, His powerful results, and His boundless blessings and rewards to flow into our lives. Appropriately, this absolutely fascinating book carries the title of the most perfect prayer we know – the one the Lord Jesus Christ Himself taught us to pray so as to impart to us the true principle of spiritual prayer.

I Can Learn to Pray – **The Lord's Prayer** – *The Prayer of The Kingdom* is for anyone who wants to know God better as "Father." The living God reveals Himself to us by the power of His love through His Son Jesus Christ – God's ever-living message to mankind. It is through the personal fellowship with Jesus Christ that we're saved from our sins and we become God's child. Christ teaches us to commune with the Father through Christ Himself, who is the Word – God's ever-living message to mankind — and He makes plain that the law of God the Father is based on our showing love to God … and to our fellowmen.

The Lord's Prayer is not only the way to knowing the will of God our heavenly Father, but also is the essential remedy for healing our soul and restoring our spiritual nature. Christ not only intended for us to say this prayer when He first taught it, but to continually live this prayer. God designed this life-changing prayer as a daily discipline for our lives – for the specific purpose of our personal spiritual growth and healing. Those who dare to believe and incorporate the Lord's Prayer into their lives will receive healing of the spirit. And when they invite Christ to come into their hearts and lives they will become a new person on the inside – born again – and will receive a new heart from God, with new desires and goals for their lives.

This book is unique for its simplicity and direct appeal to the deepest religious yearnings of mankind seeking to find "the Way" (*John 3:16-17; 14:6; 1 Timothy 2:4-6; Matthew 6:9-13 KJV*). It is, within itself, the answer to the heartfelt prayers of anyone who has expressed the dominant concern to "seek" but who has not found the One in tune with the diverse challenges and joys of their life. It points to Christ who is the road to follow, for anyone who is trying to find the way. Each chapter has instructional writings and thought provoking meditations along with inspirational quotations from the Bible, all of which is expressed in a Father-child interactive conversation.

Chapter One contains a relevant introduction intended to stimulate an awareness of God's presence with us to show the way, as well as to help the reader feel at home with prayer and with the heavenly Father. Chapters Two through Ten are grouped according to subject, with the subject of each chapter being an individual part of the Lord's Prayer. The chapters are constructed in this manner in an attempt to illustrate the true significance of the Lord's Prayer. Selecting a particular component of the prayer will enable the reader to turn quickly to the corresponding chapter to help them find certain information or inspiration to meet a particular spiritual need.

The manuscript contains an index of readings from Bible quotations pertaining to particular themes in the book. These Bible readings will help the reader's mind absorb and understand God's Word, and meditate on God the Father. It is the book's intent that countless numbers of people will be guided to renewed lives where they will be happier, richer, and nobler from hearing the good news of God's promise, and as a natural outgrowth from the wisdom gathered in these pages.

I Can Learn to Pray

The Lord's Prayer

The Prayer of the Kingdom

Our Father which art in heaven,
Hallowed be Thy name.
Thy Kingdom come.
Thy will be done on earth, as it is in heaven.
Give us this day our daily bread.
And forgive us our debts, as we forgive our debtors.
And lead us not into temptation,
But deliver us from evil:
For Thine is the Kingdom, and the power,
and the glory, for ever. Amen
(Matthew 6:9-13 KJV)

1

God shows me "the Way"
(John 3:16-17; 14:6;
1 Timothy 2:4-6)
Matthew 6:9-13 KJV

I Can Learn to Pray

The Lord's Prayer

The Prayer of the Kingdom

D o you feel that a tragic mistake you made or something you did has somehow ruined My perfect plan for your life and nothing can restore it? *(Luke 15:21)* ... You spend your time drifting in a crowded world, alone. Do you know you have a family, a common residence, the personal benefits of family life and a dwelling place? *(Luke 15:11, 24-27; John 14:1-3; Revelation 3:12, 21; 22:1-7)*. Your entire life has been a quest ... to find out who you are. Unsure of what is best, you took what you had *(Luke 15:12)* ... left home ... to be on your own ... way out into the "far country" ... far from your Father ... wherever the road will take you *(Luke 15:13)*. And oh the length you have gone ... the distance in your heart. You have no peace of mind and find no satisfaction in anything *(Luke 15:14-15)*. You begin to realize your need ... You have nothing left ... You find yourself empty ...

You're at the point of starvation, stooping to what you know is forbidden to you; you are beginning to desire what the pigs are eating ... You would have gladly eaten what was left by the "swine" *(Luke 15:16)*.

I've been searching for you *(Isaiah 53:6)*. I've been waiting for you ... My invitation to you is, "Come!" *(Matthew 11:28-30 NKJV; Isaiah 1:18 KJV; 55:1 NIV; Exodus 24:12 KJV; Genesis 7:1 KJV; Mark 1:17 KJV; Revelation 22:17)* ... Come home. Come to yourself and come to Me *(Luke 15:17-19)*. I understand your helplessness. You're a lost sheep gone astray, but I've come to show you the way *(John 14:6)*. "Come unto Me" ... and I will set you free ... I will give you rest *(Matthew 11:28-30 NKJV)*. If you're hungry, I will give you food to eat *(Matthew 4:4; Luke 4:4; John 6:35)*. If you're thirsty, I will give you water to drink *(Isaiah 55:1 NIV)*. You can come home no matter where you are *(Luke 15:20)* ... There's plenty here ... There's plenty to spare *(Luke 15:17)*. Open your heart to the gifts I AM bringing you ... All that you're longing for, have and be blessed *(Isaiah 55:1 NIV)*. You don't have to pay Me any price to get it *(Romans 3:24)*. Get in touch with Me ... I've been waiting and longing for your return *(Matthew 4:17; Luke 13:3 NIV; Acts 2:38 NIV)*.

I sit here knowing you are there. I want you to know I know the truth ...YOU could be everything you wish you could be ... if only YOU would be the hero of My story ... and return ... even when turning your back and walking away may well look easier. The amazing thing that is all true ... about you ... is that ... YOU are the child of a sovereign King ... YOU have been freely given all things ... All the gifts and blessings that come with My Salvation have been promised to YOU *(Romans 8:32)*. But you like Esau, have despised your birthright *(Genesis 25:29-34 NKJV)*. You have separated yourself from Me, and are willfully lost! But if you search for Me with all your heart, you will find Me

(Jeremiah 29:13). And if you want to become a better person *(2 Corinthians 5:17)* and to have a better life *(John 10:10)*, then YOU will have to begin where you are made (born-again a new creation), brought up ... in the "family" ... My family ... the family of God ... where you take your first step ... and come to Me ... the perfect Father who gives you *new* life *(Ephesians 2:1, 5, 8, 9)*.

Do you need a strong Father figure in your life today? Even if your mother and father forsake you, I will adopt you as My own *(Psalm 27:10 NKJV)*. You can come home to Me – I AM who I AM *(Exodus 3:14 NKJV; Revelation 1:8; Psalm 103:13-14; John 6:35; 9:5 NKJV; 14:9; Hebrews 1:1-3 NKJV)* – loving, compassionate, "Father" ... YOUR heavenly Father. You can cry out to Me, "Abba!" ... "Papa!" and I will hear you ... from anywhere in the world *(Romans 8:14-16; Galatians 4:6-7)* ... There is no length I have not gone to shorten the distance in your heart *(John 3:16-17 NIV; 10:10-11; 17:2-3 NIV)*. I could indeed display My punishing, destroying might to those who despise Me, but I choose to gently rebuke you instead ... I AM the gentle whisper in the noise, that touch your listening heart *(1 Kings 19:12 NIV)* ... Talk to Me and tell Me like it is ... With Me, You can set your secrets free. You've left home ... I know there's a solemn approaching storm *(Matthew 24:44 NKJV)*, and I have come to save you, for I must take care of my disheartened and truant child. I will never turn My back on you and leave you nor forsake you *(John 14:18; Hebrews 13:5)*. I AM someone who will stand by you wherever you are, in everything you face ... someone who will provide real-life solutions to every issue that no one else can answer *(Hebrews 13:6)*. I know I have often spoken to you before, but never in quite the same tone as I'm about to right now – "What are you doing THERE?" *(1 Kings 19:13 NIV)*.

Listen, listen to Me and eat what is good *(Isaiah 55:2 NIV)*. Everything you sought in the far country is right here at home – abundance, freedom, pleasure and satisfaction *(Luke 15:17-32)*. Learn the secret of contentment in every situation *(Philippians 4:12-13 NLT)* ... All you need to know is ...who I AM. My presence and provision will produce contentment *(Hebrews 13:5-6)*. My bread is the constant nourishment necessary to maintain your life *(Matthew 4:4; Luke 4:4 KJV; John 6:33, 35; Revelation 7:16-17; 21:6; 22:17)*. Who can take care of you like I can? ... I AM the One who knows your frame ... I know your weaknesses *(Psalm 103:14)* ... but I also know the power of your enemy. The thief – the enemy of life – comes only to steal, kill and destroy – in the end producing an abundance ... of tragic consequences. My purpose is to give life in all its fullness *(John 10:10)*. I know the things you have need of before you ask Me *(Matthew 6:9-13 KJV, 32 NKJV)* ... If you put your trust in Me, I will be your confidence *(Jeremiah 17:7)*. For I know what I AM planning for you ... not plans to hurt you, but plans to give you hope and a good future *(Jeremiah 29:11)*.

I AM loving, kind and gentle, and finding lost children is what I do, but finding one more child to fill My house *(Luke 15:4)* is My greatest joy along with keeping their lives secure. In LOVE, I choose, adopt, regenerate, care for, and discipline My children. But most of all, I speak and listen, and want to help. From the rising of the sun to the setting thereof, I love to hear many gentle voices calling Me "Father," ... remembering Me from every corner of the earth in the simple daily prayer – **"Our Father which art in heaven ..."**

I will not deal with you according to your sins nor reward you according to your iniquities *(Psalm 103:8-13)*. I want you to discover the truth of My grace ... I care more about your repentance than about whatever you did wrong ... I'd be happy — not angry — to see you return *(Luke 15:23-24)*. As a good Father, all that I want is to have fellowship with you, My child, and guide you in the new direction you may take

... so that you may find your way home to reception, reconciliation, and rejoicing *(Luke 15:24)* ... to live in new hope.

Therefore, what do I require of you, but that you come to Me ... and let Me show you the way ... to do justly, and to love mercy, and to walk humbly with the Lord your God – having the right inner attitude towards Me, and a determination to walk in fellowship with Me *(John 14:6; Ephesians 4:1 KJV; Micah 6:8 KJV)*. I AM calling you to live for Christ and walk even as He walked. It is high time to awake out of sleep. The night is far spent, the day is at hand *(Romans 13:11-12 KJV)*. Therefore, I say to you, awake! ... You who sleep ... and arise from the dead and Christ shall give you light! *(Ephesians 5:14 KJV)*. Awake to righteousness! ... And sin no more *(1 Corinthians 15:34 KJV)*.

Today, when you hear My voice, do not harden your heart *(Hebrews 3:15 KJV)* but obey My voice, and walk in all the ways that I command you, and I will be your God and you shall be My child *(Jeremiah 7:23 KJV)*. If you want to know how a young man or woman – or anyone at all – can rightly change his or her ways ... READ and HEED – by reading My Word, hiding it in your heart, then following its rules *(Psalm 119:9-11 NLT)*. My Word is a lamp to your feet and a light to your path *(Psalm 119: 105 NLT)*. Without it you can't see where you're going. Christ will teach you the way, and you will walk in His paths.

Christ is the way *(John 14:6)* ... your spiritual character which helps you to form your conscience in accordance with the truth, so that you can make sound moral choices upon which to build your life. The Spirit of Christ is your ability to reason with prudence and carefully discern and recognize the moral quality of your actions ... your obligation to follow faithfully what you know through My Word to be just and right. Christ wants to give you a total change of heart and mind with new desires and goals for your life. Christ wants to shape your moral character. He wants you to practice My commandment to love Me and love one another and make it your central moral conviction *(Matthew 22:36-40 NLT; John 13:34 KJV)*.

Christ wants to transform your life by His righteousness within you ... to do good and avoid evil by doing what is compatible with My law – loving Me with all your heart, soul and mind ... and your neighbor as yourself in a commitment to Love, Justice, and Peace. And so after Christ has done that, even though you face the difficulties of today and tomorrow, I want you to continue in Christ's love *(John 15:9-10 NKJV)* ... and obey Him *(John 14:21, 23-24)* ... Continue to do what is just and right, and live in peace with one another. And when you're wronged it can be very hard to separate your need for justice from your need for the satisfaction of righteous outrage or the need to strike back. But hear Me right ... recompense to no man evil for evil ... take no revenge against wrongs. Revenge is mine, I say *(Romans 12:17-21 KJV)*, justice is yours to do *(Deuteronomy 16:20 NKJV)*. I AM calling you to express your spiritual character in what you do – forgiving sins against Me, and sins against you *(Matthew 6:12 KJV; 28:18-20; John 20:21-23; 2 Corinthians 5:18)* ... treating your enemy kindly ... doing good to those who hate you ... loving one another as I have loved you.

All I ask is that you consider your destiny .... Tell Me, where will you be when you get to where you're going? *(Matthew 25:41 NKJV; Revelation 20:15 NKJV; 21:8 NKJV)*. Will the road you're on get you to My place? Will it get you to where I AM? *(John 14:1-3; Hebrews 11:10; 12:22; Psalm 87; Revelation 3:12; 21:1-22; 22:1-7)*. And what are you going to say when you get there? ... For I AM going to meet you as your Savior ... or as your judge. So, aren't you afraid of getting lost on the broad road to anywhere ... the one that leads to destruction? *(Matthew 7:13-14)*. Where are you now? ... Are you still trying to hide from Me? *(Genesis 3:9)*.

I've been calling you for so long that I've decided to come looking for you *(Isaiah 7:14)* ... I heard a faraway voice cry out, "Where is He?" *(Matthew 2:2 KJV)* ... and I thought that was you, looking for Me ... Be assured, I AM still looking for you. I will not rest until I take every little broken piece of you and mold you into My image *(Genesis 1:27)* ... and proclaim who you are ... My finished masterpiece of My plan and of the promise that you hold. When I say "It is done," you're now My daughter or My son. I will also proclaim "It is good ... It is very good – it is without sin ... it is YOU" *(Genesis 1: 31 NKJV),* because ... more than anything I have ever made, you are My greatest creation *(Ephesians 2:10; James 1:18; Psalm 139:14 NKJV).* You are My work of art ... You are My masterpiece ... Your Salvation is My goal *(John 3:16, 17 NIV; 17:3 NIV; 10:10).* I will create you anew in Christ Jesus *(2 Corinthians 5:17).*

Imagine what it will be like when I bring this tremendous task to a winning close, and you hear My triumphant shout "It is done!" *(Revelation 21:6)* ... when I shall keep the eternal agreement I made with you to give you what I promised when I stamped the mark of My Holy Spirit in your heart *(Ephesians 1:13; Hebrews 11:1-2)* ... and in Me you become the image that is YOU – the changeless one you're meant to be in My perfect finished plan — and your life is made secure. Then ... forevermore ... nothing shall be able to separate you from Your Father's love which is in Christ Jesus your Lord *(Romans 8:38-39),* nor from My dwelling place in the heavenly city *(John 14:1-3; Hebrews 11:10; 12:22; Psalm 87; Revelation 3:12, 21; 22:1-7)* ... which I've prepared for YOU *(Luke 15:11, 24-27)...* and you're there ten thousand years shining bright as the sun, all because of My amazing grace. I've long told you how much I love you *(John 3:16-17 NIV; 17:3 NIV).* The hour you believe in Me I will put My Spirit in your heart as a deposit, guaranteeing what is to come ... because My Kingdom comes to all. But,

I tell you the truth, no one can see My Kingdom unless he's been born again *(John 3:3,5 NIV)*.

You might have still a long way to walk before you will reach that city ... Nevertheless, I will not abandon you. I understand your helplessness – you're a slave of sin *(John 8:34)* ... You're shackled from within ... A lost sheep gone astray ... But I've sent My Son to rescue you and show you the way *(John 3:16-17; 14:6; 1 Timothy 2:4-6; Matthew 6:9-13 KJV)* ... Whoever He sets free, is free indeed *(John 8:36 NIV)*. You need not work nor fight for your liberty. You don't have to pay Me any price to get it *(Romans 3:24)*. All you need to do is ask ... and you will receive all you have always longed for ... but only if you leave your old life behind and seek the vision you barely glimpse *(Genesis 12:1-3 NKJV; Hebrews 11:13)* ... your destiny and mission ... to reach that city *(Revelation 21:24-27)* ... to be gathered in My home there ... where your spirit drink repose, the fountain of perpetual life and living flows (all the way from Calvary's mountain ... to the Holy City) ... What a place! The Holy City ... the place planned and built by Me *(Hebrews 11:10)* ... The new earth that is to be ... the final outcome of My triumphant love project for YOU ... My family ... the Kingdom of "Our Father" ... the Kingdom of My daughters and My sons.

Go tell the world the strife is over, the battle is won ... for this My daughter and that My son *(Matthew 6:10 KJV; 28:6-7 NKJV; Mark 16:6 NKJV; Luke 24:6-7 NKJV; John 20:8-9 NKJV; Revelation 5:1-14 NKJV; Revelation 21:4, 6)* ... Tell them the tempter's power is broken. The captives are free to come home to Me *(Isaiah 61:1-2 BBE; Luke 4:18 KJV)*. I have declared you are My child. Today I have become your Father *(Psalm 2:7)*. From now on ... you can come home to Me. You can find the place to where I AM *(John 14:6)*. The way to Me is through Christ Himself ... the One I sent *(John 3:16-17 NIV; 17:3 NIV)*. He is the way to where I AM.

So why do you stand there doubting ... far, far away? Wait no longer. Trust Him NOW. Turn your life in the direction of My will ... and FOLLOW ME! If you make a decided choice to follow the way to where I AM, you shall be satisfied when your vision of the city and the revelation of Me come true, and you're changed! ... And you see the changeless reality of My likeness *(Psalm 17:15; Romans 8:28- 29; 2 Corinthians 3:18; Ephesians 4:24; Colossians 3:10; 1 John 3:2)* ... in YOU ... My lamb that was lost.

Chapter

2

Our Father which art in heaven
(Matthew 6:9 KJV)

I Can Learn to Pray

The Lord's Prayer

The Prayer of the Kingdom

Father in heaven, the very fact that I can say "Our Father" lets me know I have a family. You want to have a personal and eternal relationship with me through Your plan of salvation … Through Your Son, Jesus Christ *(John 1:1 NIV; 1:14 NIV; 14:6; 1 John 1:1; Revelation 19:13 NKJV)* … The One You sent *(John 3:16, 17 NIV; 17:3 NIV 10:10)*.

You are the One true God *(John 17:3 NIV; 1 Timothy 2:4-6)*, who created all things in this universe ... including myself *(Genesis 1:1 NIV; Revelation 4:11)*. I am the very subject of Your love and Your creation *(John 3:16 NIV)*, and You have set my Salvation as Your goal *(John 3:16, 17 NIV; 17:3 NIV 10:10)* … to create me anew in Christ Jesus *(2 Corinthians 5:17)*.

You want to create in me a new nature to serve and obey You to the very end ... I ask You … How can a young man or woman – or anyone at all – change his or her ways? … You tell me "Read and heed" – by reading the Bible and heeding Your Word ... hiding it in my heart, then following its rules *(Psalm 119:9-11 NLT)*. You have dealt to everyone on earth a measure of faith *(Romans 12:3)* ... I need more faith ... Father, tell me how to get it.

Chapter

3

Hallowed be Thy name
(Matthew 6:9 KJV)

I Can Learn to Pray
The Lord's Prayer
The Prayer of the Kingdom

Our Father
which art in heaven,
hallowed be Thy name.

Y ou are everywhere and in everything the source of life
and power ... and love. Above all, Your name is HOLY.
HOLY. To You, we cannot give a holier name. Father ... Your
name is the expression of Your very essence – the actual
character of who You are. Your name is HOLY. I am the very
subject of Your love and Your creation *(John 3:16 NIV)* ...
You want me to have Your name. You want me to be HOLY.
May Your name be known everywhere, in everything, and in
everyone as HOLY ... for You are HOLY.

Nothing within my human capabilities can compare with
You: my thoughts, my wisdom, my moral standard, my position, my character, strength, ability, truth, my standard of righteousness, my patience, my capacity to love someone – none
of these qualities come anywhere close to Yours *(Romans
3:23)* You're worthy of praise, honor and glory! But, I have
chosen to disobey You and to go my own "willful" way, and
have gotten separated from You *(Isaiah 53:6)*. Yet You love
me, and You very deliberately have come looking for me
even though it has been my deliberate choice to disobey
You and go astray and gotten lost (in sin). Needless to say,
my conduct is willful and inexcusable, yet You love me and
waited patiently for me to return.

You understand my helplessness – I'm a slave of sin
(John 8:34) ... I'm shackled from within ... a lost sheep gone
astray. Yet You care so much about ME ... You have come

looking for me. You have positioned Yourself outside the door of my prison of sin and death *(Revelation 3:20)*, and though the enemy of my life is shouting, "There's no lamb here! You need not look," You know I'm in there. You're standing close to right where he has locked me in and You've let out a desperate cry ... You're calling through the Gospel ... You're appealing to my heart, to my mind, and to my will through Your love and grace ... I hear You say, "Come unto Me, and I will set you free." I long to be set free. I'm running to You ... I'm crying out, "God, help me, I'm a sinner! I've wandered away like a lost sheep ... Come and find me!"

And now, just at the right moment, You've sent Your Son to reach in and snatch me! As a Shepherd carries a lamb, so You're carrying me close to Your heart, that You may bring me back safely to You *(Deuteronomy 7:8; Romans 8:39)*. I know that I am not an easy lamb to carry, O Father. I hold Your name sacred within my heart, mind, and soul. I now know how valuable I am to You.

Father, You are holy. Outside of the sphere of Your Holy Spirit there is nothing but bondage, but where Your Holy Spirit is there is freedom *(2 Corinthians 3:17)*. I'm a slave of sin; only You can redeem me. Man's efforts cannot change me. Human wisdom cannot convert me and give me a total change of heart and mind. Only You can enter my heart and transform me from within, for You have the Word of Truth. And if I abide in Your Word, I will know the truth, and the truth will set me free ... from sin ... from this prison within *(John 8:31-32)*.

Man's law sees only my flaws and condemns me to death because of them, but Your law of love and grace gives me pardon and a life of freedom to last forever until the end of time *(Romans 7:6-25)*. Only You have the power to set me free through faith in the life-giving Savior – the promised Redeemer – the Lord Jesus Christ – Your only Son – the One You sent. And whoever Your Son sets free is free indeed

(John 8:36 NIV). I need not work nor fight for my liberty. I don't have to pay You any price to get it *(Romans 3:24).* All I need to do is ask You to come and rescue me. I don't have to pay You any price to get all I need. You tell me, "I AM the 'Bread of Life' *(John 6:35)* ... If you're hungry, I will give you food to eat *(Matthew 4:4; Luke 4:4).* If you're thirsty, I'll give you water to drink. Open your heart to the gifts I AM bringing you. All that you're longing for, have and be blessed" *(Isaiah 55:1 NIV).*

You know my fall is the devil's plan. You want me to worship You, the only true God *(John 17:3 NIV; 1 Timothy 2:5-6),* to have You as the only God in my life, and to serve You only. I ask You ... How can a young man or woman – or anyone at all – change his or her ways? ... You tell me "Read and heed" – by reading the Bible and heeding Your Word ... hiding it in my heart, then following its rules *(Psalm 119:9-11 NLT).*

Lord, You died to rid me of a life filled with sin. I guess that when I hit rock bottom, I can only look up ... to You ... There's no one else. I sense that the most exciting moment of my life is about to begin. I place my life and my eternal destiny in Your hands. Today ... I have a great opportunity to reorient my heart and to make some serious and renewing choices about where I will place my trust ... where I will spend my eternity.

With my highest honor I worship You and honor Your holy name. I want Thy Kingdom to come in my heart, so that I may partake of Your perfect righteousness by the faith You've given me – faith that fills my heart with Your love, which is the perfect character of who You are. I want Thy will be done on earth ... as it is in heaven. That You may send down into my heart deliverance instead of bondage, hope instead of terror, love instead of hate, peace instead of war, life instead of death, heaven instead of hell. For the enduring liberty of Your children has been won not by weapons of warfare *(2 Corinthians 10:4 NKJV)* the worldly savior of our carnal expectations, the means by which evil gains prominence through power, might, and force. But You won the enduring liberty of Your children by the cross. You came armed only with love – simply by the cross ... by the power of Your love through the blood poured out for us all, for the forgiveness of sins ... The blood of Your only Son ... the Lord Jesus Christ Your ever-living message to mankind ... the Savior You revealed to us. Amen. Amen.

Chapter

4

Thy Kingdom come
(Matthew 6:10 KJV)

I Can Learn to Pray

The Lord's Prayer

The Prayer of the Kingdom

Christ's divine promise to all who believe is – "I AM COMING ..." *(to deliver the Kingdom to Him who is God and Father, when I shall put an end to all rule and all authority and power - 1 Corinthians 15:24; ... when I shall make all things new - Revelation 21:5)*.

Blessed are You, our Father, God of the universe, whose ultimate desire is to forgive and bless. Your gracious promise is to send Your Son, Jesus Christ (mediator of the New Covenant – *Matthew 22:36-40 NLT*) that I might know You ... that I might let Him take the burden of toil from off my shoulders and unshackle me from the grievances of heaven *(Genesis 3:15; Hebrews 8:6-8 NLT; Exodus 20:1-17 NIV – Old Covenant)*, and save all those who believe in Him as Lord and Savior. First, He comes to take all of my sins, and give me all of His righteousness so that He might bring me back to You *(Matthew 22:36-40 NLT)* ... for He wants to put Your Kingdom in my heart – that's where it starts *(Luke 17:21 NKJV; John 14:23)* ... Then, He comes back for me ... that I shall never be separated from You again. He does not come to perform the function of "religion" but to fulfill Your inner spiritual intention – the LAW OF LOVE AND GRACE *(Matthew 5:17,43-48; 7:12; 22:35-40 NLT; John 1:17 NIV;*

3:16-17 NIV; 13:34;17:3 NIV; Romans 7:6; Galatians 3:13; 5:14, 22; Ephesians 2:1, 5, 8, 9; 1 Timothy 1:5; 1 John 3:14), which accepts me as I am but also cares enough about me to tell me the "truth" about my real condition *(Genesis 2:17; Ezekiel 18:4, 20-24; Romans 3:23; 5:12; 6:23)*, and that He intends to change me and set me free from the predicament of my sinful nature *(Romans 5:12)*. This is the truth He brings to all mankind *(John 18:37)*. All You ask is that I "believe."

I acknowledge Your Kingdom – the Kingdom that has come to earth in our hearts *(Matthew 6:10 KJV)*, and also Your Kingdom that is yet to come *(1 Corinthians 15:24-28)*. Your Word is spirit and life. Your law is love and Your gospel is peace. You sent Your Word *(John 1:1; 1:14 NIV; 1 John 1:1; Revelation 19:13 NKJV)* to show me "the Way" *(John 3:16-17; 14:6; 1 Timothy 2:4-6; Matthew 6:9-13 KJV)*. What sums up all Your teaching and ties all Your truths together is THE LORD'S PRAYER – the prayer that You taught us – the prayer of the Kingdom – Your eternal Kingdom – the Kingdom of heaven – the government of God – the Kingdom of "Our Father" *(Matthew 6:9-13 KJV)* – the house of the Lord, in which there are many mansions consisting of many nations, tribes, peoples and languages – the house in which You shall bring all of Your children together, making us one as You promised – the family of God – the righteous human race, Your dwelling place, the homeland of the saved where the righteous themselves will possess the earth, and they will reside forever upon it *(Psalm 37:29)*.

The spiritual character and quality of the Kingdom which You wish to establish in and among us, is a destiny, a mission, and a life to be carried into effect in everyone *(Genesis 12:1-3 NKJV; Hebrews 11:8-10, 13; Revelation 21:24-27)*, a Kingdom that must be proclaimed, and spread abroad to the ends of the earth *(Acts 1:8 NKJV)* ... I must prepare for it as much as You prepare it for me. United together into one body – the body of Christ, the people who have been born again and justified by His blood are led by the Holy Spirit, in their journey to the Kingdom which You're preparing for them *(John 14:2, 23)*, until finally they get there and gather in one universal assembly to remain with You forever.

In the Kingdom – the government of God, sin will no longer be tolerated and the curse will be removed. The end will come to Satan's occupation – all evil (sin and death). And You will ultimately destroy every man-made system that holds the human race in bondage. The earth shall be full of Your knowledge *(Isaiah 11:9)*, and You will forever be one with the race You have saved. You shall discern and direct the affairs of all nations *(Isaiah 2:4)*. There shall be no more separation of church and state ... because the whole world will know the truth of Your righteousness, and the only law needed throughout the world shall be LOVE – love for YOU and for our NEIGHBOR. The whole world will praise You from every nation, tribe, people and language *(Revelation 7:9-10)*, and every knee shall bow to YOU *(Philippians 2:10-11)*, and worship shall not be done merely on Saturday or Sunday, but continually to YOU *(Revelation 21:22)*. For You are the Sabbath, and You are Lord over all the earth ... and none of this will ever change.

Your universal law of love *(Matthew 22:36-40 NLT)*, along with Your unquenchable love for the world *(John 3:16-17 NIV; 17:3 NIV)* sums up the whole message that You sent through Your Son, Jesus Christ. It is the whole message of the Bible – Your ancient holy book, which reveals Your character and Your plan for mankind. Through reading Your Word, I have come to the knowledge of Your righteousness and what You require of me. According to Your holy law, everyone has violated Your will ... everyone has sinned ... none is perfect *(Romans 5:12)*, everyone falls short when it comes to meeting Your standard of righteousness *(Romans 3:23)*, everyone has failed the test *(Genesis 3:13 NKJV)*, and the soul that sins, it shall die *(Genesis 2:17; Ezekiel 18:4, 20-24; Romans 3:23; 5:12; 6:23).* You sent Your Son to tell me that You love me so much, You don't want me to die – You compel me to face the reality of my own sin and guilt, the inevitability of divine judgment, and the need for a Savior ... You have made a way for me to be forgiven *(John 3:16-17 NIV; 14:6; 17:3 NIV)* ... The ONLY way for me to be forgiven. You have given me new life through faith in the finished work of Jesus Christ on the cross.

You shall gather a people for Yourself from all the nations of the earth, a people who have been "BORN AGAIN" in Christ Jesus and justified by His blood *(John 3:3, 5 NIV),* a people who have come to You through REPENTANCE *(Matthew 4:17),* RIGHTEOUSNESS *(Matthew 5:20),* and FAITH *(Matthew 18:3)* ... In whose heart is Your law (of love) and Your gospel (of peace). And to all who receive Him and believe by faith in Him and in what He has done for us at the cross, to them You shall give the power to become Your children. They are born again, not by natural birth, nor of human passion or intention, nor by man's religious efforts, but by Your will alone – the cross of Jesus Christ *(John 1:12-13 NIV).*

And Your Kingdom shall be every place where You *are King and Your will is done. Your will shall be done in all the earth. For the Kingdom is Yours, the power is Yours, and all the glory belongs to You. Amen (Matthew 6:10, 13 KJV) ... And none of this will ever change (Revelation 11:15 NKJV).*

Chapter

5

Thy will be done on earth, as it is in heaven
(Matthew 6:10 KJV)

I Can Learn to Pray

The Lord's Prayer

The Prayer of the Kingdom

The characteristic of heaven shall possess the new earth. Your law is holy. Your will is perfect. Your Word is unchangeable. No one can change Your will *(Ephesians 1:3-10)* ...Your will is to conquer evil ... *"It is done" (Matthew 6:10 KJV; 28:6-7 NKJV; Mark 16:6 NKJV; Luke 24:6-7 NKJV; John 20:8-9 NKJV; Revelation 5:1-14 NKJV; Revelation 21:4, 6)* ... Your Kingdom in heaven shall rule over the earth ... and it shall last for ever and ever *(Daniel 2:44)* ... The power to rule over the world belongs now to our Lord and Your Christ ... and He will rule for ever and ever! *(Revelation 11:15 NKJV)* ... Forever, O Lord, Your Word is settled in heaven *(Psalm 119:89, 141, 144,151,152,160 NLT)*. The Most High will fulfil His Word ... It shall accomplish what You desire and achieve the purpose for which You send it *(Isaiah 55:11)*.

The earth as a temporal monarchy has failed Your test *(Daniel 2:44)*. Your Kingdom is come to bestow upon every man the FIFTH FREEDOM ... the final conquest of all human rights – eternal freedom from the fear of death! *(Psalm 23:4, 6; 1 Corinthians 15:26; Revelation 21:4)*. You have sent Your Son Jesus Christ to tell us the Good News, and You will not rest until Your announcement of Your Word on earth is complete, and Your Salvation comes to all mankind *(John 3:16, 17 NIV; 17:3 NIV; 10:10)* ... For it is Your will to conquer evil.

You assure me that no matter how fleeting, changeable, and unsatisfactory things may be on earth, the order of things is quite different in heaven where Your throne is – the seat of grace, the holy place from which You rule, where there is access to everything I need to take me there ... to take me "higher," that I might find Your will ... For it is the "highest" purpose in life. I must be stable, for You are stable, faithful, and everlasting and so is Your Word ... which You have sent me ... It is Your will to conquer evil ... that I might have life with You and live forever. And according to the absolute authority of Your revelation, Your will is all-important ... It will be done on earth *(Matthew 6:10 KJV; 28:6-7 NKJV; Mark 16:6 NKJV; Luke 24:6-7 NKJV; John 20:8-9 NKJV; Revelation 5:1-14 NKJV; Revelation 21:4, 6).*

Your will is all-important, ah ... Lord ... the weariness of my labor. I've barely gotten started and I'm tired already. Why on earth is life the way it is? I can't escape the ever present need to labor ... today and tomorrow ... cautiously concerned about this and that ... looking for bread, that's what ... what to eat and drink ... what to take care of in my everyday living ... and still I'm not satisfied *(Isaiah 55:2 NIV)*. I work and sweat *(Genesis 3:17-19 NKJV)* ... I try to work even harder yet to provide for my needs *(Exodus 20:8-10 NIV; Matthew 11:28-30 NKJV)*. In spite of all this, You tell me that everything I've worked for — is not my foremost need ... You tell me that my own convenience and security — is not my foremost need ... You tell me that YOU as the source of bread are more important than bread itself, and that "MAN SHALL NOT LIVE BY BREAD ALONE," but by "EVERY WORD" that proceeds out of Your mouth *(Matthew 4:4; Luke 4:4 KJV)*. You instruct me to "SEEK FIRST" Your Kingdom and Your righteousness *(Matthew 6:33)*, because

You know that my source of strength is found in OBEDIENCE to Your will ... Help me to know that as completely as You do, O Father.

You speak to me of "bread" for You are intimately and infinitely concerned about my daily bread. You call it my daily bread, but most times I call it my daily trials as well ... You know I'm not lacking for those – the trials I endure while I'm trying to find the bread. But I believe what You're saying to me is that, "The life You intend is not just about what I endure, but the bread You have in store ... for me." I believe that when You instruct us to pray **"give us this day our daily bread,"** You are also saying that You want each one of us – including me personally — to know that my inner state of mind and heart – my inner mental stability – must come from inside of me where You dwell and not from outside of me ... where I got the other kind of bread from. You want me to know that the true bread is the One You sent down from heaven *(John 6:33, 35)*. If Christ "the bread" is not inside of me, I will be hungry indeed ... I will not have nourishment for my soul – the constant nourishment necessary to maintain my life. I will not have the strength to obey Your will. For according to You, when I'm away from Your will, I cannot by myself resist the power of evil ... I'm bound to sin ... I'm a slave of sin ... I'm shackled from within ... but not only me. Though sin entered the world by one person, unfortunately everyone else has sinned as well, because every sin affects someone else ... None is perfect *(Romans 5:12)*. Everyone falls short when it comes to meeting Your standard of righteousness *(Romans 3:23)*. Everyone has failed the test *(Genesis 3:13 NKJV)*.

Sin is that which violates Your righteousness, Your will, and Your law. Sin makes me a coward and an evader, and sin leads me to seek refuge in half-truths, deceit, and evasion. Fear is the darkroom where I develop all my negatives. The awareness that I have done something wrong and of what will happen to me is more keenly on my mind than the fact that I have broken Your commandment. You demand, "Do you realize what you have done? *(Genesis 3:13 NKJV)* ... The soul that sins, it shall die!" *(Genesis 2:17; Ezekiel 18:4, 20-24; Romans 3:23; 5:12; 6:23).*

It Really Matters to You Concerning me

You love me more than anything! You made me in an amazing and wonderful way *(Psalm 139:14 NKJV).* The degree of Your personal attention on me is such that You're conscious of the smallest detail of my life. You even know how many hairs are on my head *(Matthew 10:30)* and what things I have need of before I ask You *(Matthew 6:8 NKJV).* You know when I sit down and when I get up. You under-stand my thoughts. You know all my ways ... You know everything about me *(Psalm 1391-3)* ... In fact, You write everything about me in Your book *(Psalm 139:15-16 NKJV).* You never forget me ... I'm always on Your mind ... I'm in Your thoughts at all times *(Jeremiah 29:11)* ... to such extent that You even write my name in the palms of Your hands *(Isaiah 49:16 NKJV).* You love me so much that You don't want me to die – You compel me to face the reality of my own sin and guilt, the inevitability of divine judg-ment, and the need for a Savior ... You have made a way for me to be forgiven *(John 3:16-17 NIV; 14:6; 17:3 NIV).* You have great plans for me ... plans to give me hope and a good future *(Jeremiah 29:11).* You want me to walk close with You *(James 4:8)* because You have a lot to tell me *(Acts 20:21)* ... beginning with a call to repentance from sin, and turning to faith in You.

It Really Matters to You Concerning sin

It matters to You concerning sin because sin is born of evil, which earns death. You compare the process of evil to a life cycle – with a fatal outcome. First, I'm tempted to sin .... the evil conceives from an insignificantly small thought which leads to an evil action, which gives birth to sin, and sin, when it is finished, brings forth death *(James 1:15)* ... all because ... I've yielded to temptation ... I've succumbed to my longing ... I've bowed to my will. And ... there's a terrible price to pay. You want me to come to the realization that the sin which I have committed is more serious than the price I must pay *(Romans 3:23; 6:23; Ecclesiastes 7:20; Ezekiel 18:4)* ... I am "separated" from You! You want me to have a deeper consciousness of what I have done!

This is What You Want me to Know

Sin is a choice — an *avoidable* choice that I am able to make because of the free will You have given to all of us along with Your grace. You instruct me to *seek first* Your Kingdom and Your righteousness, for my source of strength is obedience to Your will. Your *plan of salvation* outlines *Your will* on earth and Your purpose for *my life* in four simple *truths*:

FIRST ... You love me ... and want me to experience peace, have more to life on earth and that I spend it forever with You where You are. You want to have a personal and eternal relationship with me through Your plan of salvation *(John 3:16-17 NIV; 17:3 NIV; 10:10)*.

SECOND ... I am a sinner; sin has separated me from You, and there's a terrible price to be paid for sin *(Romans 3:23; 6:23; Ecclesiastes 7:20; Ezekiel 18:4)*.

THIRD ... Jesus Christ is the only answer to the problem of sin. You have provided a way for me to have a personal relationship with You through Your only Son, Jesus Christ – Your standard of righteousness. There's no other way to You except through Him *(Romans 5:8; John 14:6; 1 Corinthians 15:3-4; 1 Peter 3:18; Acts 4:12)*. He came to help me get off the broad road of life that leads to destruction, and get on Your "narrow way" that leads to life everlasting. By the free gift of Your kindness all can be put right with You through Jesus Christ, who can set everyone free from the terrible price of breaking Your law *(Romans 3:24)*.

FOURTH ... I must believe in the message of Jesus Christ, trust in Him alone to save me, and receive Him in my heart and life as my personal Savior and Lord. Jesus calls this experience the "new birth," or "being born again" *(Romans 10:9; John 1:12 NIV; 3:3, 5 NIV; 1 John 1:9; Acts 16:31; Romans 10:13)*.

This is What You Want me to do

Hear (the message of Jesus Christ), **Admit** (I am a sinner), **Repent** and **Return** (repent of all my sins and be willing to turn away from them – change my way; turn my life in the direction of Your will ... and return to You), **Believe** (that Jesus Christ is the Son of the living God), **Call** and **Ask** (call and ask Jesus to forgive me, come into my heart, and take control of my life), **Confess** (that Jesus Christ is the Son of the living God), **Be Baptized** (in water baptism and in the Holy Spirit as a sign of genuine faith and the remission of sins – remission of sins is the complete forgiveness of sins through Christ).

A simple, honest confession is what You are seeking – What You want me to do is as simple as A B C

A) Admit my need of God ("I am a sinner") and be willing to turn away from all my sins; take a turn that reorients my life in a new direction – the direction of Your will ... and return to You *(repent and return)*;

    B) Believe Your Word, that JESUS CHRIST is Your One and only begotten Son, who died on the cross and rose from the grave so my sins can be forgiven;

    C) Call on Jesus to come and help me. I'm a slave of sin – I'm shackled from within. But all I need do is *(Ask)* ask Him to set me free! ... *(Ask)* ask Him to forgive me, and to save me from the guilt of my past sins ... *(Ask)* ask Him to come into my heart, take control of my life, and trust Him alone to save me ("I want to receive Jesus as my Savior and Lord").

I must pray this prayer of repentance to receive Christ

Dear Lord Jesus,

    I have *heard Your Word.* I have come to the knowledge of Your righteousness and what You require of me. I now realize and I *admit I am a sinner.* I have sinned against You. I have violated Your will and there's a terrible price to pay for sin *(Genesis 2:17; Ezekiel 18:4, 20-24; Romans 3:23; 5:12; 6:23).* You are right when You speak and fair when You judge ... I have done what You say is wrong. I have sinned. I have played a role in my Savior's death – You died for *my* sins. It breaks my heart. I'm truly sorry. I sincerely *repent* and want to turn from my sins and follow You instead ... I want to *return* to You, and I *ask* You to forgive me, for only You can forgive sins, and I believe that You forgive those who sincerely ask You to forgive them. You love me so much, You don't want me to die – You compel me to face the reality of my own sin and guilt, the inevitability of divine judgment, and the need for a Savior ... You have made a way for me to be forgiven *(John 3:16-17 NIV; 14:6; 17:3 NIV)*.

I *believe* that You are the One and only Son of the living God. You came to help me get off the broad road of life and get on Your "narrow way" ... You came to guide me in the new direction I may take to return to a holy and a righteous God. I *believe* You took my place and died on the cruel cross of Calvary to pay *my sin* debt, to save me from the consequences of sin, and to restore my life. I *believe* You rose from the dead as the "triumphant living Lord" who has defeated the power of sin and death – the "enemy of life" – and that You hear my prayer, and You have given me new life from heaven. I *now know* that only You are my source of eternal life and my entrance to heaven. I *believe* that only through You can I be born again and have eternal life.

I change my mind, and heart, and purpose and surrender my life to Your will. Please send Your Holy Spirit to help me to obey You. I *invite* You to *come into my heart and life* and *take control*. Take control of my will, my heart, and what motivates and moves me. I *believe* in the message that You bring. I want to trust in You alone to save me, and I want to follow You as Savior, Lord, and Master for the rest of my life.

Thank You Jesus for forgiving my sins, and for saving me and giving me eternal life. Though by the law and the fair demands of a just God I'm guilty, by Your mercy I'm given a fresh start. Help me to grow in faith and knowledge of You and the Kingdom of God. I Pray in Your One and only name – JESUS CHRIST — Amen. Amen.

I must confess Christ publicly: confess that Jesus Christ is the Son of the living God

If I have **heard** the message of Christ and acknowledged Your Word; **admitted** that I'm a sinner; **repented** of all my sins; **believed** that Jesus Christ is the Son of the living God, and I have come to the knowledge of Your righteousness and what You require of me; I have **called and asked** Jesus to forgive me and come into my heart and take control of my life by praying the prayer of repentance and giving my life to Christ, then; I *must* **confess** publicly that Christ is God's Son – Son of the living God. I must declare my faith before the world as a constant testimony to the truth of the Gospel by the very life I live ... I must live Your way – making Christ known by what I am and what I do.

I must be baptized: in Water Baptism and in the Holy Spirit

Water Baptism: If I believe Jesus is Your Son and I have sincerely repented of my sins and turned to Him (born again), I must **be baptized** in the name of Jesus as an outward declaration of my conversion *(Mark 16:16 NIV)*. Water baptism is a sign that my sins are washed away by the blood of Jesus and that He has completely forgiven my sins *(Acts 22:16; Revelation 1:5)*. It publicly indicates my desire to serve You. It is a sign of genuine faith. It shows that I'm delighted to do Your will *(Psalm 40:8)*.

Therefore, I am crucified with Christ *(Christ's death)* and the person I was no longer lives in me, but it is Christ who lives in me. The new life I now live in the body, I live by faith in Your Son, who loved me and gave Himself for me *(Galatians 2:20 NKJV)*. By my baptism I died with Christ and my sinful nature was buried with Him, in order that, just as Christ was raised from the dead by Your power *(Christ's resurrection)*, so also I may live a new life and glorify You. All that the triumphant living Lord has achieved becomes mine because I put my trust in Him. Christ wants to share this victory and offer this hope to all who trust in Him *(Romans 6:4-5)*.

As Christ died once to defeat sin, and now He lives for Your glory, dear Father, so I too consider myself dead to sin but alive to Your righteousness, to live for Your glory through Christ Jesus my Lord *(Romans 6:10-13)*. My baptism is a sign that I have been made clean *(cleansing – of my heart from sin)* by faith in the Lord Jesus Christ, and that I am sincere – I have made my promise to You from a good conscience and out of a true confession *(1 Peter 3:21 NKJV)*. Therefore, in view of Your mercy and what You have done to bring about my redemption, I offer myself to You, as one who has been brought from death to life ... I offer no part of my body to sin, but rather, as instruments of righteousness ... I offer my body to You as a living sacrifice holy and pleasing as a spiritual act of worship *(Romans 12:1 KJV)*.

Father, I have done what You said I should do for the forgiveness of my sins and to enjoy fellowship with You, but I know I'm not yet able to be all You intend me to be ... I need the power of the Holy Spirit *(Acts 2:1-4 NKJV; 10:44-48 NKJV; 19:1-6)*. Christ commands us to wait until we receive it from Him ... He said, "Wait at home where you live ... where you come from ... Share Christ with those you know, and then spread out from there" *(Acts 1:4, 5, 8 NKJV)*.

The Holy Spirit Baptism: In order to overcome sin, I must have the presence and power of the Holy Spirit *(Matthew 3:11; Acts 19:1-6)*. The Holy Spirit completely satisfies every longing of the soul. The Holy Spirit gives gifts to manifest Your presence and power. These gifts will help me to share in Your very life and nature. Father, Your Word tells us to repent, change our hearts and lives, and be baptized in the name of Jesus Christ for the forgiveness of our sins, and we will receive the gift of the Holy Spirit *(Acts 2:38 NIV)*. By so doing, we are submitting to the lordship of Jesus Christ which is a definite sign of conversion and of the indwelling Holy Spirit *(Acts 9:6 NKJV)*.

The power of the Holy Spirit (also known as – the baptism of the Holy Spirit, or the gift of the Holy Spirit) is received by faith. I have surrendered my life to the Lord Jesus Christ and have a personal relationship with Him as Savior and Lord. He has entered and renewed my heart and mind and I have been made clean by faith in Him. I have repented before You, God my Father, and given up all my sins to You. I know that if I ask You, Heavenly Father for any one of Your promises – such as the baptism of the Holy Spirit, I am confident that You will give it to me. For You said in Your Word, "... How much more shall the Heavenly Father give the Holy Spirit to them that ask Him?" *(Luke 11:13 NKJV)*. I ask You now to fill me with the power of the Holy Spirit. By faith, I believe that You have granted it to me.

Now that You've gained entrance and made me Your temple *(1 Corinthians 3:16 NKJV)*, You proceed to empower me with the Holy Spirit for living and growing in faith, which prepares me to continue Your plan before You send me out into the world to witness. After receiving the power of the Holy Spirit, I will have divine guidance and enabling from You in the presentation of the Gospel, and boldness to witness to everyone everywhere of Jesus' death and resurrection – the good news of Jesus which proves Your love for mankind and all that You have done to bring about our redemption *(Acts 1:8 NKJV)*. The Holy Spirit – the Spirit of truth which convinces the world of sin, righteousness, and judgment *(John 16:8-11; Acts 16:29-30 NKJV)*, will testify of Jesus *(John 15:26 NKJV; 1 Corinthians 12:3 NKJV)*, and lead me into all truth *(John 16:13)*.

The power of the Holy Spirit will enable me to be effective for the Kingdom of God, especially if I have a desire to do my best in seeking to follow Christ anywhere He leads me – to the place where He will bless me *(Genesis 12:1-3 NKJV)*. When I offer my self to Christ with a willing heart, in return He will give me countless gifts to keep and gifts to give away *(Ephesians 4:11 NKJV; Romans 12:3-7 KJV; 1 Corinthians 12:1-12,28 NKJV)*. Because I love Him, He will empower me to accomplish tasks which are far beyond my human powers and abilities. He will empower me to do the things I never felt I could. If by faith, I continue to walk with Him and discover His Word, I will find direction for my life. He will help me learn to do well. He will help me discern and interpret my abilities, know my strengths from my weaknesses, know right from wrong and good from evil so that I will know what's evil and ought to be avoided, and know what's good and ought to be done. He will help me to declare Your truths, and have the gift of the Holy Spirit's abiding presence in my life – the fruit of the Spirit – love, joy, peace, patience, kindness, goodness, faithfulness, gentleness, and self-control. There is no law forbidding the possession and practice of these virtues *(Galatians 5:22-23)*.

This enabling power from You will help me to obey Your law in its true spiritual intent *(Exodus 20:1-17 NIV – Old Covenant; Matthew 22:36-40 NLT – New Covenant)*, and will instruct me to see the need to live and be led daily by it. You reward any one who earnestly seeks You *(Hebrew 11:6)*. Your gift is to every one that is "born again" of the Spirit *(John 3:8 NIV; Acts 2:39 NIV)*. This new birth from heaven – this great change made in the heart of the sinner by the power of Your Holy Spirit, is something done in us and for us which no one else in the world but You could have done for us. The gift of Your Holy Spirit is given to me as a sign of the power and authority from You to my repentant heart, and it enables me to become totally converted so I can worship You in spirit and truth, and overcome sin.

But for unbelievers who do not seek Your pardon and forgiveness, they do not have the gift of Your Holy Spirit to keep them in line, and what the sinful nature does is quite plain. It shows itself in immoral, filthy, indecent actions, and evil thoughts and desires. People become enemies and they fight; they become jealous, have selfish ambitions, outbursts of wrath, divide into groups and factions causing dissention and discord; they become envious and have feelings of ill-will; they commit adultery, fornication, murder, get drunk, have orgies, and do other things like these. Some people even worship idols, and indulge in witchcraft. Such life-style is proof that one has not become a new creature in Christ. Those who do such things will not inherit the Kingdom of God *(Galatians 5:19-21)* ... unless they genuinely repent.

Father, You said that I may slip-up and fall into these sins, but I will be miserable until I confess and forsake them. But thank God, I belong to Jesus. I have nailed the passions and desires of my sinful nature to His cross and crucified them there. A listening ear to hear what You say will give me controlled strength to gain mastery over sin. And a life of faith lived consistently with the Holy Spirit, will produce the fruits of the Spirit – love, joy, peace, patience, kindness, goodness, faithfulness, gentleness, self-control and much more *(Galatians 5:22-23)*. With qualities like these and the countless gifts You give, I can match any task and capable of overcoming any difficulty.

I am Now a Citizen of Your Kingdom

Father, You made the world ... including myself. Your glory is the example of Your love to the world ... and Your love for me. You are the WORD (the Greek word *logos* – *John 1:1 NIV)*. You sent Yourself – the living WORD – to guide me in the world. You sent the Word in the form of a person to tell me what to do *(John 1:14 NIV; 1 John 1:1; Revelation 19:13 NKJV)*. You love the world so much that You sent Your One and ONLY Son JESUS CHRIST – the "LIVING WORD" — so that anyone who believes in Him and trusts Him to save them, shall have eternal life *(John 3:16-17 NIV; 17:3 NIV)*, and not eternal death awaiting them. He tells everyone, "Come to Me and I will give you the bread of life. I AM "the bread" sent from heaven. Come and get all You need ... get whatever You can't live without" *(John 6:33, 35)*. The ones who believe and come to Him to receive it, He will never, never turn away *(John 6:37 NIV)*. His sheep hear His voice and follow Him, and You give them eternal life – they will never die *(John 10:27-28)*.

Your Kingdom, the heavenly government, will rule over the entire earth and will bring endless blessings to those who obey You by accepting Your Son Jesus Christ as Lord and Savior *(Matthew 4:23)*. Your standard of righteousness is in the person of Jesus Christ *(John 1:14 NIV)*. Instead of a list of rules to govern Your Kingdom, You sent Him to show us Your character and nature. You sent Your Son because You want to give me an accurate image of who You are as well as set an example of Your Kingdom – what it is, what it will do, how I can receive its blessings, and how I can share the "Good News" to everyone.

I am now a citizen of Your Kingdom and as such, I now live for Christ, not because of any self-seeking behavior or an effort to follow a canonical list of do's and don'ts written in stone or on a piece of paper, but because of Christ in me – Your law of love written in my heart – the reality of Your love and forgiveness *(Romans 7:6)*.

Your Kingdom is come on earth – and in my heart. The driving force of my life is to do Your will. When I admit my need of You, turn away from my sins, and pray the prayer of repentance, Christ's Spirit becomes my own. I am changed from within. His Spirit helps me to realize that I cannot say *"our"* if I only live for myself. I cannot say *"Father"* if I do not endeavor each day to act like Your child. I cannot say, *"Who art in heaven"* if all my interests and pursuits are earthly things. I cannot say, *"Thy Kingdom come"* if I'm unwilling to accept Your will, but continue to sit on the throne of my heart ... not getting off of it ... not allowing You to rule me from within.

I don't want sin to reign anymore in me ... I want You to *(Romans 6:12-14)*. I don't want sin to any longer be enthroned in my heart, nor be the ruling power within me ... I want You to. I don't want to live by the weariness of labor or by bread alone, but by every Word that comes from Your mouth. I must read Your Word every day, believe Your truth, and act upon it.

Transform me inwardly so that Your will is done in me. You have set my salvation as Your goal ... to create me anew in Christ Jesus. I am so glad to know there is such a God as You whose ultimate desire is to forgive and bless. Now I have hope for each day. I will do Your will to do the things You plan – to carry out into my heart and life, and into the consciousness of all people the name JESUS – the only One who can liberate the soul from the shackles of sin and then give the promise of salvation – new life within.

Things I Must Practice Daily for Spiritual Growth

Father, after I've given my life to Christ, turned my life in the direction of Your will ... and return to You, there are four things You want me to practice daily for spiritual growth. I must:

- **Pray** – I talk to You
- **Read my Bible** – You talk to me

- **Witness and bring others to Christ** – I talk for You
- **Stand firm to the end** – I must hold fast to Your truth, and build a strong spiritual foundation

I must be faithful in prayer – I talk to You

Prayer lets me get close to You. The prayer of salvation is my first real conversation with You. It is the genuine outcry of my needy heart. I want to come and talk to You about the deep issues of my heart. I want to tell You that I acknowledge that Jesus Christ is Your Son; that He came to earth as a man in order to live the sinless life I cannot live. I confess my past life of sin and not obeying You. I also want to talk to You about my deep, constant, and daily needs, my hopes, dreams, joys and everything else that is important to me. I want to tell You about my thoughts, desires, hurts, and problems, as well as give You thanks and praise. I want to ask You for more faith to trust in You, obedience to abide in You, and patience to wait on You. I acknowledge any particular sin I have done and I ask You for continued spiritual growth and cleansing.

I must confess, I love to come to You about myself – about what "I" want to be ... even though I know that You're busy working on Your plans to mold me into what YOU want me to be ... always, I just want to talk to You about ME. But though I love best to pray to You in private (mostly about me), I discover that prayer is much more than just about ME ... I'm reminded of how You taught us Your children to pray: "*Our* Father ... Give *us* ... Forgive *us* ... Lead *us* ... Deliver *us* ..." I know now, that united prayer is important to You and is essential to us – You want Your children to come together, as Your Spirit leads, to lift up their hearts to You in confession, adoration, thanksgiving, petition, intercession, and supplication.

As a believer, You want me to not just pray and read my Bible, but also to associate with other believers by being part of a community (a local church) where a person receives the help, support, correction, rebuke, encouragement, and fellowship needed to live a successful Christian life, and the opportunity to minister to others. The local church is Your institution on earth to equip me to "GO" into all the world. The local church must be Bible-based. It must be a body of believers who can teach me Your Word, and provide spiritual growth, and partnership to accomplish Your work in the world *(Hebrews 10:25; Acts 2:42, 47 NKJV; 5:12-13; Philippians 1:5; Matthew 16:13-18; Ephesians 1:22, 23).*

You want me to continually come to You in prayer, but my prayers must not only be about me and my circumstances. You want me to have a community focus – be inclusive of others – praying for my family, the church (believers everywhere), the local community, the country, and the world, and You even want me to pray for my enemies too *(Matthew 5:44).* I must give You a more important place in my prayers than I give to my personal concerns. In fact, dear Father, in order to change me, You seek to gently bend my will so that it gradually takes the shape of Your will and thus ultimately Your very nature and purpose.

My foremost expression in prayer must not only be about my own convenience, but for the rule of Your Kingdom on earth in the hearts of all people *(Matthew 6:10).* I must grieve for the human anguish of the lost and pray earnestly for those who have not yet come to faith in You. I must also pray earnestly for believers everywhere ... that they may have Freedom of Speech to boldly tell others of Your law of love and Your divine message of peace with God *(Ephesians 6:18-19 NKJV).* For in some parts of the world, there is fierce persecution for those who come to believe in Your message and those who spread the Gospel. My prayer must be an act of total confidence and assurance in Your plan and purpose, so that Your will may be done on earth.

But while I pray for sin to be removed, I must also pray for all sorrows to be wiped away. My obligation is to speak up for those who cannot speak for themselves *(Proverbs 3 1:8 NIV)* ... Do justly and have mercy and pray for the poor and the afflicted ... and if needs be, to work on their behalf, and to seek justice for everyone *(Isaiah 58 NKJV)* ... You tell me, "That which is altogether just you shall follow" *(Deuteronomy 16:20 NKJV)*. You give me the example of Your prayer — **"Our Father which art in heaven ..."** so that I may grasp the true principle of spiritual prayer. Soon, Your Holy Spirit will teach me how to lay hold of Your willingness to help me do Your will and use my gifts, talents, and resources to accomplish a lot of good things for You in the world. So Father, I know it is important that I keep an appointment with You everyday to talk to You in prayer.

I must read my Bible – You talk to me

I read ... You tell me ... "Incline your ear and hear ... A person lives not on bread alone, but on everything I say *(Matthew 4:4; Luke 4:4 KJV)* ... If you abide in Me, and My Words abide in you, you will ask what you desire, and it will be done for you" *(John 15:7 NKJV)*. The deep importance of this truth becomes clear when I begin to understand that Your Words in me are the equivalent of Yourself in me. My inner state of mind and heart must come from inside of me where You dwell and not from outside of me. You want me to know that if You're not inside of me, I cannot have the strength to obey Your will. And if I stay in You, hear Your Words, and obey Your instructions, You'll give me what I ask in line with Your will. For Your will brings wonderful blessings *(1 John 3:22 KJV)* ... All the gifts and blessings that come with Your salvation have been promised to me. I can come to You and get whatever I ask for, because I have chosen to obey Your instructions and do what pleases You.

Father, I have tried my best to find You – please help me not to wander off from what You've told me to do. I have given a lot of thought to Your Words, and kept them in my heart so that they would hold me back from sin *(Psalm 119:10-11 NLT)* that I might live a new life in You. Oh, how I need to pay attention and hear, for every solution I seek is found only in You ... But oh how I need to help others to know You, so that they will hear too and live happier lives. And, oh how much my power to speak (to someone else) depends on that of hearing You! For You call us to be Your witnesses, to say – *this is what I've seen ... this is what I've heard ... this is what I know about Christ.* And so, I wake morning by morning to hear You *(Isaiah 50:4-5)*, and to ask You to help me to speak (declare Your truth), but also to understand, stay in You, and obey Your commands. You have opened my ears, and I just want to live so that I can hear You and let your laws help me.

Without faith no one can please You. Anyone who comes to You must believe in You, and constantly seek You and not wander away *(Hebrews 11:6)*. Those who love Your instructions will have great peace, and nothing can entice them to sin or wander away. Nothing can make them stumble *(Psalm 119:165 NLT)*. I remember when I used to be Your disobedient and wayward child with feet set to wander ... out of the way. But I've come to my senses, and come to You .... The perfect Father who has given me new life *(Ephesians 2:1, 5, 8, 9)* Paying attention to Your instruction gives me peace, it gives me hope, it gives me a better life. Why turn away from something that gives me hope. Why turn away from something that is my very life? You loose me from my bondage and set me free *(Matthew 11:28-30 NKJV)*. You want me to stay free so that I can enjoy my freedom from slavery to sin *(Romans 6:18)*.

As long as my foot is fixed firmly on to the pathway of Your Word *(John 14:6)*, You'll see to it that nothing can unfasten it – for You don't want me to go astray and get lost ... it is not Your will for me to perish *(Matthew 18:12-14 NKJV)*. I am Your little lamb that was lost ... You know me well. You know me from head to toe. You know how hard it is to find me when I wander away. You keep my foot locked for You want me to be safe and sound. You keep my feet from wandering because You want me to come home safely to You. You're a God and Father who not only make known Your Word, but enrich those of Your children who confide in it, and honor and obey You – You have given me a better life.

Thank You above all else, that sin reigns no more in me – You reign *(Romans 6:12)* ... Sin is no longer the ruling power within me ... It is no longer enthroned in my heart – You are. You have dethroned the power of sin. I will recognize You for who You are ... You must increase ... and I must decrease *(John 3:30 NIV)* ... for You are holy. Now that Your Kingdom has come – in my heart, I will no longer sit on the throne of it. I'm getting off for You to rule me from within ... My will is not my own until I make it Yours. I submit myself to You for Your will is good – it is the only good one ... I will abandon my will ... I only want what You want. As in heaven, so on earth, Father ... Thy will be done ... I must surrender to You and then I will be free. Choosing to serve You is a wise thing to do. In fact, You tell me that it is my obedience to You that proves I have mastered the first elements of wisdom – godly intelligence – understanding truth, and the ability to discern right from wrong *(Psalm 111:10; Proverbs 1:7)*. You tell me that if I lack wisdom in anything all that is needed is simply to ask You for it *(James 1:5)*. So, I'm on my way. And sure enough, I'm going to pack my bag with my favorite book – Yours ... I'm going to read it and continue on … continuing in the things that I have learned of You *(2 Timothy 3:14)*.

From reading Your Word — the Holy Scriptures — I know about the many good things You have in store for those who love You, and I know what You expect from me. I know now that I must not live by bread alone, but by every Word that comes from Your mouth. I must read Your Word every day, believe Your truth, and act upon it. I must "read and heed" and follow Your Word … I must hide it in my heart so that I might not accidentally or willfully sin against You *(Psalm 119:11 NLT)*. For Satan carefully calculates how to influence my thoughts *(Genesis 3:1 KJV)*, because he knows that as a man thinks in his heart, so is he *(Proverbs 23:7 KJV)* … and whatever that man thinks, that's what he's going to do. So, let me set my eyes on Your Word and start thinking right … and be transformed by the renewing of my mind *(Romans 12:2 KJV)*, so that my actions will begin to develop … then my life will begin to change.

Therefore, I will spend some time getting my mind lined up with Your Spirit so that I can know You and know how to obey You. I will diligently search the Scriptures to understand Christ as my personal Savior, to discover Your truth, to correctly interpret what You have said in order to make sound moral choices, and to chart out a straight course for my life. I will keep an appointment with You every day to study Your Word. Today, I will read three chapters from the Bible. I will begin from the book of John because I want to know and believe that Jesus Christ is Your promised Son, that believing in Him I might have eternal life *(John 20:31 NKJV)* … because eternal life is knowing You the only true God, and knowing Jesus Christ whom You have sent to earth *(John 17:3 NIV)*. I will then read Psalm 119, and 1 John, and continue from there.

I must witness and bring others to Christ – I talk for You

The true response of one who has found Christ is to bring others to Him. I must be a witness and GO and TELL others THE GOOD NEWS of Your Salvation. I must regard every person with a view to his/her salvation and instruct him/her concerning the same *(John 1:41 NIV; Matthew 28:16-20; Mark 16:15 NIV; 2 Corinthians 5:18-21; John 20:21)*. You call me to be a witness, to say – *this is what I've seen ... this is what I've heard ... this is what I know about Christ.* I must declare my faith before the world as a constant testimony to the truth of the Gospel by the very life I live ... I must live Your way – making Christ known by what I am and what I do.

Entrusting my life to Christ is an act that requires commitment *(John 14:15)*. That means, I must not sit casually and just be a believer – a branch *(John 15:2 NKJV)*. A believer must become a disciple – a branch bearing fruit *(John 15:5 NKJV)*. A disciple is one who has confessed his sins, repented of his sins, and received Christ in his heart – to put it briefly he's "born again" *(John 3:3,5 NIV)*, AND ... has made a radical decision to deny himself and take up his cross daily and follow Christ *(Luke 9:23 KJV)* ... continuing to believe, and living as Christ tells him to *(John 8:31-32)*. And no one has to beg the disciple to give up a little of anything. He gives up everything ... including his prior commitments ... to follow Christ *(Acts 2:44-47 NKJV)* ... He obeys Christ in everything *(John 17:6 NIV)*. He comes to the point where he even hungers and thirsts after Your righteousness *(Matthew 5:6)* ... seeking to know You better. For You are the water and the bread of life. And if the disciple abides in Jesus – the Vine – he will bear much fruit. For Christ and the cross are the source of life *(John 15:5, 7 NKJV)*. Jesus rightly says that no one can be His disciple unless they first sit down, count the cost of all they have, and then renounce them all for Him *(Luke 14:33 NIV)* ... and, that anyone who wants to follow Him must deny himself, take up his own cross daily, and follow Him ... with unrelenting determination *(Luke 9:23 KJV)*.

Yet, His rules are fair *(Psalm 119:7 NLT)*, and He cares so much for me. For as He asks me to take up my cross and follow Him, so He beckons me to cast my crushing burdens upon Him *(Matthew 11:28-30 NKJV)* ... so that He can help me carry them ... so that He can show me how to carry them. For He knows that it isn't the weight of the cross that loads me down, but the way I carry it ... I must come to Him and learn from Him and let Him help me ... His yoke (of authority) is easy – He is gentle and humble and kind, and gives me only light burdens. He promises me rest when I'm tired ... He gives me a break and sets me free. His yoke is easy because His commandments are not meant to burden me down but to lift my burdens off. And as He makes my burdens lighter, I find that I can't live without the cross ... Without the cross, I would be lost.

In all things, Jesus who died for my sins, is worthy to receive power, and riches, and wisdom, and strength, and honor, and glory, and blessing *(Revelation 5:12)* ... including that special place in my heart. I can never ascribe too much to Him ... He is worthy of my obedience, my love and devotion, and all else. For not only has He proven that only the love of Christ can illustrate the extent of what love is through the nature of God's love for every one of us, but that He – the Lamb who was slain and who was raised to life again – is able to conquer evil (sin and death) to secure the present safety and the eternal salvation of humanity, and to assume responsibility of the future of all mankind *(Revelation 5:1-14 NKJV)*.

We can put our trust in Him because only the love of Christ has stood the test of time. In actual fact, we can leave our old lives behind and follow Him anywhere He leads us ...

to the place where You will bless us *(Genesis 12:1-3 NKJV)*, because He is worthy to be believed, for He has triumphed – He has passed all the tests, and in His life, death, and resurrection all the prophecies have met their fulfillment. And Father, we can count on You with our very lives. For You have given us the opportunity to trust You. For in Your Kingdom there is PROVISION, PROTECTION, FORGIVENESS, and now DELIVERANCE – You so loved the world that You made such a sacrifice to have given Your one and only Son, that whoever believes in Him should not perish but have eternal life *(John 3: 16-17 NIV; 17:3 NIV)*.

Christ has triumphed and He wants to share this victory and offer this hope to all who trust in Him. And if we believe Him, we must love Him. If we love Him, we will give up all and follow Him. We will invite Him to come into our hearts and stay. And when we do, His indwelling Holy Spirit will do things in our heart, soul, and mind that will bring us to a place of oneness with You, dear Father *(Matthew 22:37-39 NLT; John 14:15)*. And if I dare to believe and incorporate Him into my life, I have found not just my Master, but my freedom *(John 8:31-32, 36; Romans 7:6-25)* ... I have found "the One in tune with the diverse challenges and joys of my life" *(John 10:10)* ... The One that lifts my burdens off and gives me a break ... The One that looses me from my bondage and sets me free *(Matthew 11:28-30 NKJV)* ... He's the reality of Your love and forgiveness. In Him, I have found my very life! ... The One that I've been searching for. I will want to do the things He loves – "Your will" to accomplish Your plan and program in the world – to conquer evil and save those who believe in Jesus Christ as Lord and Savior *(Revelation 21:6)*, and set us free from sin and death *(Romans 8:2)*.

Christ wants to enter our hearts and to transform us from within by His Word of truth. Christ in me – Your law of love written in my heart, is the reality of Your love and forgiveness *(Romans 7:6)*. This transformation translates to faith, love, and obedience that helps us show the way *(John 3:16-17; 14:6; 1 Timothy 2:4-6; Matthew 6:9-13 KJV)*. This kind of faith will surely lead us to GO and TELL the Good News – saying, **this is what I've seen ... this is what I've heard ... this is what I know about Christ** ... leading others to the Lamb who shed His blood on the cross to save us ... helping them to know Christ ... bringing them into Your presence to receive the peace, joy, and hope that You offer through Himself the Lamb who was slain and who was raised to life again to give new life to all people everywhere.

And as we go, we are compelled not by law, but by our new nature within us – our love for You and others. We now want to exhibit consideration and kindness for others, as well as forgiveness motivated by unselfish, sacrificial love and mercy. We "follow the Lamb wherever He leads us" to share our faith in word and action to that someone somewhere. That someone could be an outcast leper, a deadly insurgent, a convicted murderer, or anybody who needs to hear about the amazing love of the heavenly Father. The assignment could be a pleasant or a dismal one, as close by as next door, or as far away as some remote, forgotten corner in the uttermost part of the world. But Jesus said, "If you love me, 'do it' ... keep my commandments" ... He's worthy of all that He requests. So Father, I will keep an appointment with You every day to tell someone about Jesus who has given me new life in Him, that they too may believe and be blessed. I will not let Your message comfort the people in their sin – I will not distort and refute the true message of God to the detriment of the people. And most of all, I will not pervert Your sacred trust for personal enrichment. But I will make my heart right with You my God Jehovah, and give to You what is rightfully Yours *(Zephaniah 3:4 KJV)*. Amen.

I must stand firm to the end

Father, according to Your Word, it is very important that I build a strong spiritual foundation *(1 Peter 2:5; Romans 6)*. I must stand firm and hold on to the truths You have taught me. I must remain faithful to You, holy in life and character, and true in communicating Your Word in my actions *(2 Thessalonians 2:15 NKJV; Revelation 2:25-26; 3:7; 21:7)*. Now that Christ has set me free, I must stay free and don't let myself become a slave to sin anymore *(Galatians 5:1)*. I must stand up as a free person, and begin to walk with Christ my leader and instructor, until He becomes my constant companion. I must keep walking on a straight path, be committed to live a faithful Christian life, and stand firm to the end *(Matthew 10:22; Mark 13:13; 1 Corinthians 15:58)*.

Because of inherited imperfection, all human beings struggle to do whatever is right. A guilty conscience can easily lead to doubt, fear, discouragement, and self-reproach, and it makes us feel inadequate. But You assure us that when we ask Jesus to forgive our sins and help us to live on the right side of Your law, we can maintain a good conscience before You, which gives us peace of mind and promotes dignity, well-being, and a sense of value, which contributes to our happiness and brings blessings into our lives. You said that when Jesus forgives our sins, we learn how to live our lives in a way that benefits us and brings praise to You. Why? Because when we prove our love by obedience and allow Jesus to rule us from within, that is when **"Your Kingdom has come"** in our hearts. And where the Spirit of the Lord is, there is freedom ... liberation has come *(2 Corinthians 3:17)* ... I'm free from the bondage of sin ... I am free from the prison within because I have accepted Your Word – I have accepted Your truth – I have chosen to believe in Christ's forgiveness and let Him in to help me take the burden of toil from off my shoulders and set me free ... make my burden lighter ... so I can stand tall *(Matthew 11:28-30 NKJV)*. With Christ my leader and instructor, Your truth will give me the wisdom to see where I'm going, and the power to understand how to get there – by following the Master Teacher – Christ Your living Word.

Because I have surrendered my life to Christ, I am saying, **"Thy will be done on earth, as it is in heaven"** ... I am saying, I am truly ready to give myself to Your service here and now. When I pray **"Thy will be done,"** I am anchoring my eternal hope in the promises of Christ my Savior, thereby acknowledging that You are in complete control of my life, that You love me with unlimited love, that You have good intentions for me, and that You desire true happiness for me. I can set my mind at rest now because ... for sure ... Your will is going to bring wonderful blessings and help me to be what I ought to be – standing tall.

By Your triumphant victory at the cross, You have the adversary right where You want him ... under my feet ... where he belong *(Romans 16:20 NKJV)* ... I must never let him get to my head where he can influence my decisions ... I must put on **the helmet of Salvation** which You gave me *(Ephesians 6:17 NKJV)*, when I came to You with my heavy burden *(Matthew 11:28-30 NKJV; Acts 2:38 NIV)*. I must never let him get the freedom to use the new mind You've given me. Your truth will set me free *(John 8:31-32)*, but his lies (traditions, false teachings and theories, and commands of men) will hold me captive and put that burden of toil on my shoulders again *(Galatians 5:1)* ... and I don't want to be his slave anymore – bending low.

I must stand tall. I must spend some time in getting my mind lined up with Your Spirit. I must bring into captivity all the thoughts of my mind to obey You *(2 Corinthians 10:5 NKJV)* ... I must conquer every thought with Your sword (of the Spirit) ... the *Spirit*WORD – **the Word of God**

(Ephesians 6:17 NKJV) ... What's more, I must not let my heart (nor my head) be troubled *(John 14:1)* ... I must not let anything throw me into confusion – I must release all doubts and fears. I must be strong and not doubt, but believe. I must stir up my faith in You. What You have already perfected in heaven I must bring forth on earth ... both in my heart, and in my mind – where I am free to serve Christ who is Your living word on earth and my example to show me the way.

I must begin to live the victory You have started at the cross. I must bring forth that victory into my heart – where Your Kingdom on earth starts, and in my mind where it carries on. For I'm raised up together with Christ! ... I'm being changed to be like Him *(2 Corinthians 3:18)*. As Christ was victorious over the power of sin, so I too may walk in this victory by the power of His Holy Spirit which He has given me ... I must live by faith ... I must walk in victory! *(Galatians 3:11; Hebrews 11:1)*. When You say I can do something *(Philippians 4:13 NLT)*, I must not let the adversary tell me I'm not able to, or that he won't let me obey You. The minute I begin to live like a champion that's when he's going to try me out ... with defeat. So now, for sure, the enemy is going to test my armor.

When he comes at me, I'm going to need to know what to do. I need to understand my enemy, learn how to fight, get me an armor, and know how to wear it. But this time I'm going to need to get the whole armor for no ordinary weapons will do. You want me to put on the whole armor – full protection from head to toe, for the enemy will use everything to attack me *(Ephesians 6:11 NKJV)*. You give me some powerfully built spiritual weapons to fight him with. After I'm all set and geared up, You call me out for inspection ... You command me, "Fighter! You have enlisted as a soldier of Christ. Go get your whole armor. Stand! Take **the band of Truth** – the revealed Word of God – and put it around your thighs ... Walk around with true integrity and sincerity, and let your weapon be always in plain sight ... Soldier! ... Walk in victory! – that is, if you obey Me no matter what" *(Ephesians 6:14 NKJV)*.

You give me the **breastplate of Righteousness** – my protective covering and body armor, my bulletproof vest to shield my character and conduct. You tell me, "Now, put this on. You're going to need it everywhere you go" *(Ephesians 6:14 NKJV)*. With **the preparation of the Gospel of Peace**, You put on my shoes and prepare me to GO ... and do Your will ... making known the Good News of Your salvation to everyone everywhere – saying, this is what I've seen ... this is what I've heard ... this is what I know about Christ *(Ephesians 6:15 NKJV)*. You say to me, "Here, take **the shield of Faith**. Now, he (the enemy) is not just going to be after your character and conduct, but after your very life. This shield will put Me between you and him. In his efforts to destroy you, I will stop anything he throws or shoots at you ... I'll not only stop the weapons but put out the fires ... I want you to know, I'll stop the guided missiles of that misguided foe" *(Ephesians 6:16 NKJV)*. You give me **the helmet of Salvation** to protect my head (from traditions, false teachings and theories, and commands of men), so that I may have confidence and boldness in the fight, and conquer every thought with the sword (of the Spirit) ... the S*pirit***WORD – the Word of God** ... for the battlefields of the mind *(Ephesians 6:17 NKJV)*. Because when the enemy comes after me, I'm going to have to know what to do.

I'm a warrior ... on my own out here on this great big battlefield (of life). I have my sword (the Word of God). But to get assistance, I must do everything by **Prayer**, asking You for help *(Ephesians 6:18 NKJV)* ... **praying always** as I engage in battle ... keeping the lines of communication open with Christ the Captain of my salvation. When the battle gets hot, I must fight hard with my communication weapon (prayer) along with my revealed weapon (my sword

don't let me be put to shame! I will pursue Your commands, for You expand my understanding. Teach me Your decrees, O LORD; I will keep them to the end. Give me understanding and I will obey Your instructions; I will put them into practice with all my heart. Make me walk along the path of Your commands, for that is where my happiness is found. Give me an eagerness for Your laws rather than a love for money! Turn my eyes from worthless things, and give me life through Your Word. Reassure me of Your promise, made to those who fear You. Help me abandon my shameful ways; for Your regulations are good. I long to obey Your commandments! Renew my life with Your goodness" (Psalm 119:30-40 NLT).

The Word that was with You Father, is now with us *(John 1:14 NIV)*. Your Word in heaven is now on earth – we can know You! I can know what is good and do what is right, and become my best self. The highest good is to be born from above into Your holy Kingdom. You help me understand not just what is, but what ought to be. For You have a plan and a purpose for my life. May Your will be done on earth in my heart, just as Your will is done in heaven where Your throne is – the Seat of grace, the holy place from which You rule – where there is access to everything I need to take me higher, now that I've accepted Your will to find my "higher" calling and the "highest" purpose in life … in Jesus name. Amen. Amen.

Today, I ask God's forgiveness, turn from my sins, and accept Jesus Christ in my heart and life as my Savior, Lord, and Master.

My Name: _____

Time of Day: _____ Day: _____ Month: _____ Year: _____

I Will

Your Sovereign Goodness

Father, although in life we may sin and directly hurt one another every day, all of our trespasses ultimately hurt You. This grieves Your heart *(Ephesians 4:30; Psalm 95:10 NKJV)*. For we have strayed away like sheep and have left Your paths to follow our own way *(Isaiah 53:6)*. And since You're a just God, every wrongdoing has to be accounted for. Sin is the willful transgression of Your holy law. And, according to Your law, the soul that sins, it shall die *(Genesis 2:17; Ezekiel 18:4, 20-24; Romans 3:23; 5:12; 6:23)* ... Unfortunately, everyone has violated Your will ... everyone has sinned ... none is perfect *(Romans 5:12)*. Everyone falls short when it comes to meeting Your standard of righteousness *(Romans 3:23)*. Everyone has failed the test *(Genesis 3:13 NKJV)*, but You will not rest until Your salvation comes to all mankind.

What is salvation? ... It is Your sovereign goodness, which saves us from the death penalty – the end result of unforgiven sin. Though we neither easily obtain forgiveness from one another, nor do we easily give it to one another, yet it is for our forgiveness sake that You, through Your sovereign goodness, have sent Your Son to earth to die for us, and take our place. Thank You God, He did. Otherwise we would have to fulfill that part for ourselves – and it would be all over ... eternal death would be ours forever! But Your sovereign goodness, the grounds for my redemption, has sent a Savior, Your Son JESUS CHRIST to die in my place, and pay the full and complete payment for the penalty of my sins, so that whosoever believes in Him, desires to be forgiven, and sincerely accepts Him as Lord and Savior, will not perish but have everlasting life *(John 3: 16-17 NIV; 17:3 NIV)*.

The startling question is, why ... in spite of Your sovereign goodness, do we always transgress Your holy law? Mankind has come a long way. So, how could we have come so far but still be in the same place ... of sin? How could the story of what is happening on earth in the time of the Universal Declaration of Human Rights be just like the one that happened in Paradise? ... Well, that's easy ... the earth is full of Satan's temptations! ... and the willful transgression of Your express command. "But don't you see," some may say, "We have our 'freedom' and 'liberty' ... It protects our 'human rights' ... It protects us from everything ... and everyone everywhere." To that You'd respond wholeheartedly, "But not from Satan your enemy." Real freedom and liberty is a life controlled by Your truth and motivated by Your love. And when it comes to our *sin nature* and "What on earth is happening!" ... It never changes – It's always a l-o-n-g story, full of Satan's temptations ... and the willful transgression of Your express command. Your law and man's liberty are at enmity with each other ... But Father, You're going to change all that *(Ephesians 1:3-10)* ...

A grasp of that truth would be incomplete without the moral of my story. And I will tell my story, so that all who still might not know about the good news of Your *salvation*, might also know about the tale of the one (mankind) who has come so far but is still in the same place – of *sin*, because it is every one's story too.

Well, let's start with me – I have come a long way. My birthplace was no Paradise ... but I was still in the same place – of sin, and here's what befell me ... For the cause of Human Rights and national and international unity, the Universal Declaration of Human Rights in its concept of "Natural Law" affords me FOUR FREEDOMS – freedom from want, freedom from fear of human aggression, freedom of speech and expression, and the freedom to worship You – God, or not at all. And of course, I went for the "not at all." Each of these freedoms supports the whole which is suppose to give me liberty anywhere I am. But still, the "enemy of life" (the power of sin and death) would try his best to snatch freedom and liberty away from me and leave me shackled from within. He would not leave me alone! He pursued me everywhere and became more aggressive every day. I was a slave to sin ... I tried to do everything that would gain his approval. But he used every means available to mislead and manipulate me. He would offer me "advice" and instead I would find it to be "a vice." By temptation he used every word to interpret my destiny – he tells me, "You know ... let me be honest with you. They call me a thief and a robber *(John 10:10)* ... but you know I'm not. You don't have to run from me. I know how I can change your life forever ... I'll show you how – if you would just work with me a little ... I'll pay you *(Romans 6:23)* ... I'll give you freedom and liberty ... I'll give you everything you want ... an abundance of everything you want!"

But somehow, that "abundance" is an abundance ... of tragic consequences. Somehow, that "everything" about that thief is just to get a blank check ... to do as he pleases ... and get everything HE wants from me, while he takes an oath and signs me a promissory note to pay me "something" he swears to give me *(Romans 6:23)*. He's the enemy of life – that wicked serpent ... He's sin and death! ... But what's this "something" he swears to give me? What's this 'Just work with me a little'? What's this request? What does that mean? I wish I knew. What will he pay me? Sounds too good to be true. I want to know more! I want the truth! ... As I searched his eyes full of lies, to my delightful surprise, he whispers in my ear, "Don't worry, I'm going to pay you ... in full *(Romans 6:23)*. Then ... with a subtle hiss, he added ... "S-s-slave!"

By then I realized I would have no real freedom unless I was free from sin. I knew he should pay me ... But, I could not trust him in anything at all ... especially since I found out that the only truth in his word is the "I'm going to pay ..." So one day, I took matters in my own hands and did what I could to defeat him. Armed with the weapon of moral uncertainty, I soon became a coward and an evader. I sought refuge in half-truths, deceit and evasion ... I did what I could to survive ... trying to find my way ... trying, trying with all my might ... trying to find the sense of staying right. But before long, nothing could change my wandering ways. I became a "lost sheep" ... "dog" ... I was baa-a-a-d. I was GUILTY! And in no time at all, the enemy of life began to control me, acting like he owned me. He kept me hungry and thirsty and always seeking to be satisfied. He gave me no rest and never provided for my needs. I needed food, but the price was high. I went looking for water, but the well was dry. I was a wandering sheep ... I had no one to guide me. Then one day he burst out, "You're NOT FREE!" *(Genesis 2:17; Ezekiel 18:4, 20-24; Romans 3:23; 5:12; 6:23)* ... But somehow I already knew that ... so there go my 'freedom' and 'liberty' – the one he promised me. They didn't last very long, did they? Then, he put a dreadful PRICE tag on my head and took me to the marketplace – called life ... to sell me ... to sin! ... And there I met my Savior *(Romans 3:24)* ... And anyone can add their storyline to mine ... But the moral of the story is that: all the stories conclude the same – "You're NOT FREE!" All (mankind) are under the bondage of sin. The only hope is the Savior *(Galatians 3:22 NKJV)*.

Now, the story of Adam and Eve ... that was a great tragedy! They lived in Paradise, only to lose it! One was tricked and the other made a deliberate choice to disobey You and reject Your authority, and thus got in trouble with Your Law. So far, it was not a pretty sight over there in Paradise. Adam and Eve were evicted from their Eden home and it was protected from them ever returning. They did not just lose their Eden home. They lost original justice, AND ... for the rest of their lives they lived without it ... exiled by their sin, soul cast down within, separated from You, as they marched out of Paradise and took the pathway to sin, into a decaying world full of thorns. You, Almighty God, demanded of them, "Do you realize what you have done? *(Genesis 3:13 NKJV)* ... The soul that sins, it shall die!" *(Genesis 2:17; Ezekiel 18:4, 20-24; Romans 3:23; 5:12; 6:23).*

The sad thing, Father, is that Adam and Eve started the whole thing – transgressed Your law by committing the first sin AND ... caused the first death! ... by eating a piece of fruit! One act of disobedience to You was sufficient to allow sin to enter all of us ... and death began to rule! – It had the final word. Whether or not it was a small act of disobedience, or whether or not it was disobeyed just once, the bitter fact is that sin has its consequence – death! Adam and Eve conceived the "sin nature" ... then passed it on and there I was ... guilty as well ... facing a death penalty! ... for an unforgiven debt I couldn't even pay ... And no one could set me free ... But that was before I met the Savior ... Now death no longer has the final word ... the triumphant living Lord does. Wish they had never tasted the fruit of any kind of sin ... But I'm not going to blame them — my original "parents" — for anything. The truth is, I was guilty because I knew that sin is not merely the unavoidable condition of being human; rather, it is an avoidable choice ... but I chose to disobey You anyway. I was not personally guilty for what they did, but for what I did. I knew I was breaking Your law but I ran from Your correction – let Satan tempt me – and I did it anyway *(James 4:17; 1 John 3:4)* ... for just like them (my original parents), I was not righteous. I was not perfect. I needed Your help. I needed You to come and rescue me.

But, You're awesome! You're altogether lovely, and Your mercy endures forever. I worship You for who You are. You came by the marketplace. You took one look at me and knew I was in big trouble ... Sin and death got hold of me ... I couldn't get away ... I couldn't pay (my sin debt, that is to say). It got real messy. But You wouldn't leave me in that condition. You promised to send me a Redeemer *(Genesis*

3:15; Hebrews 8:6-8 NLT; Galatians 3:13) to pay the price to redeem me from the hands of the enemy (sin and death), and bring me back to You. This Redeemer is the *only* One who could get me out of the mess *(John 1:14 NIV)*, that I may be free to come in Your presence again. *You* paid a price to buy me out of the slave market (of sin) and stamped on my sin debt "PAID IN FULL." Wow! I was happy. You set me *free*! ... thrust the "Living Document" of freedom (the Word of God) in my hand! ... and made my mess a message ... You entered into my very heart and cut the shackles of sin. And oh, the intoxicating taste of freedom! I got out of there so fast and headed in the new direction You showed me to go *(John 14:6)*, to find Your eternal Kingdom.

You bought me back! I'm not up for sale anymore, and I will never have to go back to the marketplace. I will never have a ridiculous price tag on my head again. I will never have to return to that bondage. Along with the name of THE LIVING GOD whom I serve, I now have the word "VICTORY!" and "ENDURING LIBERTY!" along with the name "THE LIVING GOD whom I serve" *(Galatians 6:17)* stamped right over the place where my sin debt had been stamped. My heart is free, my mind is free, and my will is free, I'm free from all fear, I'm free from all want, because I'm a partaker of YOUR **enduring liberty** which lasts freely available and for all times. I have been given the 'Living Document' of freedom (the Word of God) from Christ – the Giver of life Himself, and I'm free to worship You ... and tell everyone about it. The law of the Spirit of life in Christ Jesus has made me free from the law of sin and death *(Romans 8:2)* ... I have ENDURING LIBERTY! ... I have VICTORY! over the enemy of life. I will never have to fear him anymore. His power is broken! I will never have to fear the thought, "AM I FREE FROM SIN?" I will never hear the word "GUILTY!" I'm now under new ownership and management. I am free to obey You, keep Your laws, love and serve You with a clear conscience ... for the rest of my life!

Your Universal Law of Love and Grace

You gave Your law (the old covenant) which governed Your relationship with Your people when You took them by the hand and led them out of the land ... of bondage. You instructed them, "I AM giving you My commandments to keep. You are to make My Word a priority. They are to be upon your heart. They are to be taught and learned. You are to talk about them when you sit at home and when you walk down the street, when you lie down and when you get up. Nail them to the doorways of your homes. Write and post them up everywhere, and carefully teach them to your children" *(Deuteronomy 6:6-9 NKJV).*

You wrote Your law (the old covenant) in stone and gave them these ten specific commands – a set of moral rules to keep. You reminded them: "I AM the Lord your God, who brought you out of Egypt, out of the land of slavery. 1) You shall have no other gods before Me; 2) You shall not make for yourself an idol in the form of anything; 3) You shall not misuse the name of the Lord your God; 4) Remember the Sabbath day to keep it holy; 5) Honor your father and your mother; 6) You shall not murder; 7) You shall not commit adultery; 8) You shall not steal; 9) You shall not give false testimony against your neighbor; 10) You shall not covet" *(Exodus 20:1-17 NIV).*

The law was their teacher to tell them what was right from wrong. But evil was too strong for them to overcome on their own. The law demanded perfection but could not provide it. For fulfillment of the law was through faith in Yeshua Messiah – Your living Word. Out of the goodness of Your heart, You changed the rules and offered to come Yourself and bring Your Word – through Yeshua Messiah.

You would provide a better hope than the law. Faith in Yeshua Messiah is called "The Better Hope" which is called "The grace of God." Though faith in Yeshua Messiah the people could draw near to You, get to know You, and walk with You *(Hebrews 7:18-19 NKJV)*. Through that better hope, You would bring them to Yeshua Messiah to remove the penalty so that they would be justified – declared innocent – not guilty. That better hope through Yeshua Messiah would defeat sin – bring Salvation – new life within. The Holy Spirit would bring conviction to the hearts of the people so that they recognize their sin. The Holy Spirit would open their eyes to what they had done wrong.

You told them, "Look! I AM giving you a choice. You can choose life and good, or death and evil ... I call on heaven and earth to witness this day that I have given you a choice between life and death, blessing and curse. Therefore, obey My commands and choose life so that you and your descendants may live" *(Deuteronomy 30:15, 19 NKJV)*. You told them that Your overall plan is that they trust in the good news of Your promise to send Yeshua Messiah – Your Son, Jesus Christ as Lord and Savior (mediator of the new covenant), to save those who believe in Him to remove their heavy burden (of sin) and change their lives forever *(Genesis 3:15; Hebrews 8:6-8 NLT)*, and that when He comes, You would put Your law in their minds and write it on their hearts *(Jeremiah 31:33 NKJV)*.

You gave Your law (the old covenant) to restrain sin, but sin defeated Your law – no one ever kept it – they were unable to walk in perfect obedience and righteousness before You. The people broke it all the time, and sin held them in bondage. Then they learned that law alone ... written on stone ... cannot make someone perfect and righteous ... it cannot give someone a willing spirit. Law serves to show someone where they are wrong, and make them conscious of sin so that they realize what they have done, but it cannot remove the penalty and declare them "not guilty" ... it cannot save anyone from sin or change them from within *(Galatians 3:22-24; Hebrews 8:7)*. Law measures us against the perfect life that we're called to lead, but it cannot make us perfect. People lacking the Holy Spirit are incapable of wholehearted obedience. People need a new heart and a new spirit within to enable them to internalize Your law, to love it and obey it with willing and eager hearts *(Deuteronomy 6:25 NKJV)*. The law was not there to pardon and forgive. Pardon and forgiveness comes through Christ alone *(John 1:17)*. The law was there to convict them of sin, and show their need for a Savior who would change them from within, and change their lives forever. Your law (the old covenant) prepared them for Your promise (the new covenant) which was to come – the Messiah.

But when Your Son, the Savior, Jesus Christ (mediator of the new covenant) came to save us as You promised, He nailed sin to the cross, defeated sin, offered me pardon and forgiveness, and set me free! You mold Your law into a new and beautiful covenant of "love and grace" through the Holy Spirit, which serves as a guide to lead me to a personal relationship with You through Christ, and to restore fellowship with me – Your most precious creation.

Your covenant of love and grace – the reality of Your love and forgiveness *(Romans 7:6)* – now writes Your law not externally – in stone – but internally in my mind and heart, and my thinking and motives, and transforms me into Christ's image. Your covenant of love and grace governs my relationship with You and establishes the foundation for relationship with one another. Your covenant of love and grace states that of supreme importance and priority are – my responsibility to God, and my responsibility to man. Your whole law hangs on two commands: 1) I must LOVE YOU, and 2) I must LOVE ONE ANOTHER, namely, I must love You with all my heart, all my soul, and all my mind – I must love You with my whole being. This is the first and most important command. And the second is equally important: I must love my neighbor as myself *(Matthew 22:36-40 NLT)* ... My neighbor is anyone who needs my help ... especially those who are the most difficult to help ... my enemies.

But no law can save me. It cannot give me perfect standing before You – a holy, perfect, righteous judge. All my own efforts to keep the law or live up to it will not bring me up to Your standard of righteousness. It is only when in repentance I ask for forgiveness and new life, through Your grace, that I'm justified (declared righteous – innocent – not guilty) by faith in Jesus Christ and I'm saved (from the death penalty). Through Your Son, Jesus Christ (mediator of the new covenant), I'm compelled not by law, but by my new nature within me to love You and one another, and to keep the law (the New Covenant – *Matthew 22:36-40 NLT*; the Old Covenant – *Exodus 20:1-17 NIV)*. I am no longer under the law of do's and don'ts written externally in stone (the old covenant) which You gave to restrain sin, for sin reigns no more in me! ... I live by it, but I'm no more under it, because the power of the Holy Spirit (through Jesus Christ) which changed my heart gives me the power to live above it.

The purpose of the law (the old covenant) was to expose sin, but the purpose of Your Son, the Savior, Jesus Christ (mediator of the new covenant) is to defeat sin. You sent Your law of love and grace to earth to work together as a rescue mission team in bringing salvation in Jesus Christ to rescue helpless sinners. Whereas the law convicted me of sin, declared me guilty and showed my need for a Savior, Your grace worked as a life jacket or life preserver that You my Father threw out to me when I was sinking deep in sin, so that when I reached out and caught hold of it by faith, and accepted Jesus Christ in my heart and life, He saved me. He saved me by giving me forgiveness of sins and eternal life.

He paid the full and complete payment for the penalty of my sins. Now, through the power of the Holy Spirit which changed my heart, all who reach out and take hold of Your grace have a new power that defeats sin. Through Your grace, Your Holy Spirit empowers me to live by the Spirit, and I will not gratify the desires of the sinful nature *(Galatians 5:16)*. And as Christ was victorious over the power of sin, so I too can walk in this victory by the power of His Holy Spirit which He has given me. For Your Word declare, "The just shall live by faith" *(Galatians 3:11)* – not by law ... No human being can live in his own power the true intent of the law (the New Covenant – *Matthew 22:36-40 NLT*; the Old Covenant – *Exodus 20:1-17 NIV)*. That requires a life of grace which comes from God alone ... This is something which only God can give. Christ living in me is my only hope of a life that pleases You, dear Father *(Galatians 2:20 NKJV)*.

You're not prejudiced or partial, nor are You blind to my faults, and yet You call me "holy." You call me "accepted." In Your view, what I was is not so important as what I may become. You love me in spite of who I am or what I've done. I've been hungry and thirsty and seeking to be satisfied in the wrong places. But You fill me up and provide for all my needs *(Psalm 23:1; Genesis 48:15; Numbers 27:17 NIV; Revelation 21:6; 22:17)*. You are the water and the bread of life. Now when I hunger and thirst, I hunger and thirst after You and Your righteousness. You love me with such a great love, I know You will not withhold any *good* thing from me. Once I knew of Your great love, I no longer doubted Your provision nor ran from Your correction – because everything that You do is for my *good.*

I am not an easy lamb to lead, but still You watch over me and correct my wandering ways. You lead the way and when I stray You bring me back. You give me instruction in righteousness – an inner principle to guide me that I may not lose my way again *(Psalm 23:3)*. Dark valleys or not, I'm not afraid of getting lost, for You lead the way *(Psalm 23:3)*. You lead the way for me and call me to follow You ... wherever You go ... for the rest of my life *(Revelation 14:4 NKJV)*. You're always out in front facing the danger so that the dark valleys are no longer a place of fear to me ... You make the path safe. Your rod and staff comfort me *(Psalm 23:4)*. You protect me with Your rod, which is the Word of God. Your staff is the cross ... there's nothing like it to guide me and draw me back to You ... For there's nothing like the love You demonstrated to bring me back safely to the fold when I wandered and strayed.

You lead me with care and bring me to a place of quiet rest where I spend a lot of time with You *(Psalm 23:2)*. Some might call You the Good Shepherd *(Psalm 23:1)* ... but Lord, I know that You're not only good ... You're great! ... You're the Great Shepherd ... You are my guide and the One who takes care of me ... You provide for me and restore my soul *(Psalm 23:3)*. My survival depends on You – You will defend me and lay down Your life for me no matter what *(John 15:13 NKJV)*.

The enemy of life is the king of terror to a little lamb like me. He knows I'll win through Jesus, but he does not want me to believe it. So, he tries to scare me. I tell him I know all about it because I read it in The Book – the revealed Word of Truth. One time when I continued to proclaim the victory and I reminded him of the blood of Jesus and how Christ rose to new life again, the enemy of life got so scared – he began to sweat ... because it reminded him of his defeat at the cross. So, he postponed it and waited for a better time to come at me.

Yes, the enemy of life is the king of terror to a little lamb like me, but not to the Great "life-giving" Shepherd. You see the enemy of life coming and You're not even afraid ... And that calms my fear ... for it's not for lack of trying why he hasn't snatched me ... But while You're armed with the rod and the cross, he will not venture near me ... he will not dare pursue me when I have the Word of God for my protection. Observing Your rod and staff security switch on, he just turns and walks away ... that comforts me ... that strengthens my faith ... that gives me peace ... that's how I'm able to walk through the darkest valleys. Despite the menace of the years (the enemy of life), You keep me, and keep on keeping me unafraid. That gives me hope!

Because I've decided to walk with the Shepherd who rescued me, He adopts me as His own *(Psalm 27:10 NKJV; Romans 8:15; Galatians 4:6-7; Ephesians 1:5)* and wills to me all He has, and all He has achieved. He reassures me that I will live with Him forever! ... in His home – the one He's gone to prepare for me ... The one He's building to move me into. That will be my permanent residence *(Psalm 23:6; Philippians 3:20; Luke 15:11, 24-27; John 14:1-3; Revelation 3:12; 21; 22:1-7)*. Whether I deserve it or not, You cause goodness and mercy to follow me all my life *(Psalm 23:6)*. What a comfort to know Your provision and love. Your goodness makes me enjoy life even more.

I have sinned and broken Your law, and thus I deserve to die. One day, I received a solemn message – I must come in to court. I must appear before You right away. I'm under sentence of death. The date of my trial is set. The proceedings start. In the Book of Life which You hold in Your hand, are written all the things I've ever done. Everyone is standing there ... ready to hear. I'm brought face-to-face with Christ, the Righteous Judge, the One in whom I've trusted – the One You sent to save my life – the only One who can save me. He opens the book. He searches for my name. Suddenly, I hear a great voice shout, "Don't bother to look. You're not going to find it." With glee, the loud-mouth enemy of life reminds everyone, "The name's not there! But where's he, anyway?" Afraid of death, I began to sweat. In intense agony, I watch as the enemy ignores me ... ignores my pain, ignores my shame, ignores my fear of eternal doom ... all the time reproaching me, accusing me, condemning me, repeating again and again ... "The name's not there!" Then as I wish for a mysterious miracle – a place I could hide, or the imperceptible moment I would disappear, or become invisible and sneak out of there, and no one could spot me at all ... he spots me ... and turns a threatening gaze at me, yelling, "Hey! You, standing alone over there ... You who always prayed for your sins to be forgiven and faithfully trusted in the only One who can save you ... Tell us how you missed the mark! ... Tell us why you're standing there ... Tell us why you failed! ... Is there any hope for you now 'lawbreaker'? ... All set to hear the word GUILTY? ... Ready to pay the never-ending penalty? The 'Living Document' of freedom YOU received some time ago when you received your salvation and trusted in the One to save you, is no longer yours ... How I longed I could get my hands on it – your salvation award – life itself! Now, I have it! ... It's over here ... in MY hand!"

Then to make matters ten times worse, he steps up to me and whispers in my ear, "Hey you ... I know you ... I know that you have faithfully trusted in the Lamb who shed His blood on the cross for you – the only One who can save you. And YOU even tried to conquer me by the message of your testimony of Him. YOU have the mysterious energy of Christ that dared you to advance against me the tempter. But oh that what I wish, would come upon you! ... That you've really messed up now! ... And that your slate is not clean."

With all the holy discipline and reserve in Christ, He ignores the rude interruption and continues His search. Then, in a moment of triumph, Christ shouts, "Look! The name is here!"... And with ever-reigning VICTORY, Christ snatches the Living Document of freedom – my salvation award – life itself – from the enemy's hand! ... Removes the penalty ... Declares me NOT GUILTY! ... Throws the case

out of court at the bar of divine justice ... Puts my salvation award – life itself, in my hand and bestows upon me the Fifth Freedom – eternal freedom from the fear of death! *(Psalm 23; John 10:11-18; 27-30; Hebrews 13:20-21; 1 Peter 2:25; 5:4; Revelation 7:16-17). Hebrews 13:20-21; 1 Peter 2:25; 5:4; Revelation 7:16-17).*

Then I heard a loud voice shouting, "It has happened at last! ... Now have salvation and power come, and the Kingdom of our God and the authority of Christ, His anointed One. For the enemy of life – the accuser of all those who trusted in Christ Jesus, is defeated and cast out. Christ has dealt the decisive blow to him and defeated his power over sin and death. Christ has destroyed his authority over the kingdoms of this world. And both he and death will never come back again ... He accused those followers of Jesus day and night before God! But they conquered him by the Covenant of the blood of the Lamb shed on the cross, and by the message of their testimony ..." *(Revelation 12:10-11).*

Triumphant Living Lord, all the attempts of that wrong-doer have proven unsuccessful against me ... and fatal to him! ... Because, Your Kingdom has come! ... in my heart, and on earth. Your goodness has saved me from the death penalty! You have declared me righteous ... innocent ... not guilty! You, the perfect author – author of my life, author of my salvation, and author and finisher of my faith – have wiped my slate clean and written a new story about me. You have written me up for something GOOD! You have written my name in the pages of Your holy book for everyone to see *(Revelation 20:12 NIV).* With Christ's redemption, He the ultimate ruler over all the earth – the Giver of life Himself – the One in whom I've trusted – has snatched enduring liberty and the Living Document of freedom (the Word of God) out from the hand of the conqueror and enemy of my life and have bestowed upon me the FIFTH FREEDOM ... the final conquest of all human rights – eternal freedom from the fear of death!

You promise to all of humanity Your "universal law of love and grace" *(Matthew 5:17,43-48; 7:12; 22:35-40 NLT; John 1:17 NIV; 3:16 NIV; 13:34; Romans 7:6; Galatians 3:13; 5:14,22; Ephesians 2:1, 5 8, 9; 1 Timothy 1:5; 1 John 3:14)* if we will just let You point the way *(John 3:16-17; 14:6; 1 Timothy 2:4-6; Matthew 6:9-13 KJV)*. And, Father, all may come into Your presence and offer themselves to You, just as I did *(Acts 2:38-39 NIV)*. You do not come to perform the function of "religion"... You erect no doctrinal barriers between You and man. You do not impose upon us any convincing, any preliminary studies, any great scholarship or knowledge of letters, any intellectual theorizing or even preaching. All Your "religion" consists in believing the mysteries of the cross and the One You sent. A simple, honest confession is all You are seeking from us.

Sharing the Great Triumph of Life

Your law and man's liberty are at enmity with each other. Real freedom is a life controlled by Your truth and motivated by Your love. Ever since Adam ... well, of course Eve too ... she's not without blame. Remember? Someone lied to her – she was tricked – but I was just stupid ... I thought I had a better way than Yours. So ever since Adam made a deliberate choice to disobey You, reject Your authority, and get in trouble with Your Law, his disobedience (original sin) brought Your judgment down on all mankind. You demand, "Do you realize what you have done?" *(Genesis 3:13 NKJV)* ... "The soul that sins, it shall die!" *(Genesis 2:17; Ezekiel 18:4, 20-24; Romans 3:23; 5:12; 6:23)*. The penalty for this disobedience (death) was to be borne by each succeeding generation *(Romans 5:12)*.

All had sinned and broken Your law *(Romans 3:23)*, and there was no escape from the death penalty *(Romans 6:23)*. The end result of unforgiven sin is eternal death. But according to the doctrine of justification, which has its origin in Your sovereign goodness – the ground for our redemption, You – the holy, perfect, righteous judge – have removed the death penalty so that we're declared innocent – not guilty. You gave us an opportunity to find life in Your Son, Jesus Christ who is faithful and just to forgive us our sins, and to cleanse us from all unrighteousness *(1 John 1:9)*. Your love has provided a Savior *(John 3: 16-17 NIV; 17:3 NIV)* – the Messiah, Jesus Christ, Your promised Son, Son of Righteousness, the full and complete payment for the penalty of our sins, the Obedient One, the sacrificial Lamb to die in our place, the Good Shepherd, the just One, the Prince of Peace, the second Adam and our example. You gave Him the free will to either choose His own way or to do the will of You, His Father, who sent Him. But thankfully He surrendered to Your will.

Because of Christ's obedience, by Your power He was crowned with life on resurrection morning. Christ defeated the power of sin and death – the enemy of life! The power of sin over all our lives has been canceled! Christ has ensured our eternal life. Now, at last, Your Kingdom (the Kingdom of God) has come in our hearts to be our example to show us the way. Christ, Your promised Son, has dealt the decisive blow to death! Christ's substitutionary death in our place has satisfied the demands of Your justice, thereby enabling You to forgive and save all those who place their faith in Him *(Romans 3:26)*. Christ has paid mankind's debt to You. The slate is wiped clean. Man is truly free at last! ... But Father, not too many people know about this *free, priceless gift* that You have willed to them as Your beneficiaries, and are still running from Your correction. Yet, there's no time to lose ...

They need to come and claim it *now* before it's too late. The time to claim is running out!

This priceless gift is the Good News You send to mankind: that You have purchased a pardon for us so we don't have to be on the run anymore. You have given us FREEDOM IN CHRIST, and EVERYONE CAN COME and have their sins forgiven *(Galatians 5:1)*. There is no eternal doom awaiting those who trust Christ to save them *(John 3:18 NIV)*. Every time we sin (break Your law), we are covered by the sin offering of the "Lamb of God" — Your Son, JESUS CHRIST, whose sacrifice is the only One You accept. Through the redemptive and propitiatory sacrifice of Jesus on Calvary, the believer is made righteous and reconciled (bought back) to You, completely and irreversibly freed from the guilty verdict of sin. This means that You acquit us and declare us "NOT GUILTY" of sin and death *(Romans 3:23-24; Galatians 3:13; Ephesians 1:17)*. What an awesome declaration for any fugitive to hear! I must spread the Good News to everyone everywhere ...

Your urgent message to everyone is, *"You must be born again"* to be a part of My Kingdom – the Kingdom of God" *(John 3:3,5 NIV)*. You give each person *"new birth"* when he or she receives Jesus Christ as his or her personal Savior and Lord. Upon being *"born again"* the Christian receives *new life* from heaven – Your gift of everlasting life. Your Kingdom comes on earth in the believer's heart *(Matthew 6:10 KJV)*, and in Your earthly reign yet to come *(1 Corinthians 15:24-28)*. The person who comes to Christ becomes brand new on the inside, changed in his moral nature by the regenerative power of Your Holy Spirit. A new life begins! *(2 Corinthians 5:17; Ephesians 4:24; Colossians 3:10; Galatians 6:15)*. The believer is thus enabled to separate himself from sin *(the corrupting influences of the world)*, become consecrated in You *(dedicated to the service of God)*, and sanctified *(cleansed; changed in nature; redeemed by the power of the Holy Spirit; made pure, free from sin, declared holy and acceptable in God's eyes).*

With his eyes fixed on Jesus, the believer now offers his life to You as a sacrifice with a sense of obedience in his heart and life to Your plan as he heads in the new direction You show him to go. Like a proud loving Father, You call out to him, *"Child, remember the first and most important command – you must love the Lord your God with all your heart, soul, and mind ... and the second is equally important – you must love others as much as you love yourself (Matthew 22:37-40 NLT) ... If you love Me, obey Me" (John 14:15).* Whether or not a child takes direction joyfully or reluctantly with a sigh, You know that somewhere ages and ages hence, their obedience is going to make all the difference. For love is that narrow path that leads to the Kingdom, and no one can say they love You and hate Your commandments. No one can say they love You and hate someone else *(1 John 4:20-21 NIV; 1 Corinthians 13:1-3, 13).* You want every one of Your children to return in full the love You have for them. For the measure of their love for You is their love for others.

We can put our trust in You because *only the love of Christ* has stood the test of time. Only the love of Christ can illustrate the extent of what love is through the nature of Your love for every one of us. The amazing grace that expresses the heart of the heavenly Father is the change You long to see in the world. Christ is LOVE. This is THE KINGDOM OF GOD that You want to come within our hearts. Your standard of righteousness is in the person of Jesus Christ *(John 1:14 NIV).* You sent Him to show us Your character and nature. Christ does not lead with hate in order to overthrow with might. Christ is the One who, by His example, has shown us how to love one another. He tells us that we cannot love You unless we love our brother. Christ is the One who multiplies fish and bread, not swords and spears ... the One who does not slaughter the enemy, but heals his wounds ... and raises him from the dead. He is the One You sent to restore our lives, save us from the wrath of Your indictment, and change our destiny *(John 3:16 -17 NIV; 17:3 NIV; Romans 4:5; Matthew 22:37-39 NLT)*. Only Christ is the One who has reconciled with You on our behalf, and who has shown us how to reconcile with one another *(Isaiah 2:2-5)*.

Christ communicates Your love for all people and looks for goodness and faith in everyone, even those dwelling in unexpected places. In Him we see truth, justice, integrity, hope, faith, peace, love, and righteousness in their fullness, and suddenly we see who we were destined to be. He wants to move the whole of humanity on its way to this fulfill-ment through Love, Justice, and Peace. For CHRIST is THE PRINCE OF PEACE and the promise of redemption to humanity *(Isaiah 9:6-7; Psalm 2:7; Acts 13:29-39; Luke 2:14)*. And He who is the mighty God and Lord of eternity will be a benevolent Father, bringing a peace that will be eternally established in His Kingdom. And that's what Christ communicates. Christ wants to bring peace so that Your name will be honored, Your will done, and there will be just individuals, just leaders, just laws and fair dealing nationally and internationally. Christ is in contrast to the ever present "mutually assured destruction" (MAD) which the enemy of life promises to every human soul *(Galatians 5:15)*. Christ comes armed only with love – simply by the blood of the cross. His law is love and His Gospel is peace. Christ knows what it means to be human – He knows we're not perfect – He comes to show us the way *(John 14:6)*. He comes to aid us so as to prevent our destruction. Christ's love has the prin-ciple that can truly ensure the future for those who would let Him shape it *(John 3:16 -17 NIV; 17:3 NIV)*.

Thank You, Father, that Jesus not only died for my sins but that He is alive today at my side forevermore – the TRIUMPHANT LIVING LORD — hearing my prayers and my every word, preparing a home for me in anticipation of Your Kingdom on earth, and making my life secure. Not only has He proven that only the love of Christ can illustrate the extent of what love is through the nature of Your love for every one of us, but that He – the Lamb who was slain and who was raised to life again – is able to conquer evil (sin and death) to secure the present safety and the eternal salvation of humanity, and to assume responsibility of the future of all mankind *(Revelation 5:1-14 NKJV)*. We can put our trust in Him because only the love of Christ has stood the test of time. In actual fact, we can leave our old lives behind and follow Him anywhere He leads us … to the place where You will bless us *(Genesis 12:1-3 NKJV)*, because He is worthy to be believed, for He has triumphed – He has passed all the tests. Christ wants to share this victory and offer this hope to all who trust in Him. Accepting Christ is sharing THE GREAT TRIUMPH OF LIFE! All that He has achieved becomes mine when I put my trust in Him. In trusting Him, I'm poised on a new threshold of opportunity! In faithful commitment to You Father, I trust and abide in Your promises *(Psalm 119 NLT)*, for You are my source of "bread." You supply me daily.

My "bread" is the daily personal realization of Your presence with me. It is nourishment for my soul – the constant nourishment necessary to maintain my life. When I have this I have all things. It helps me to develop and possess a spiritual strength that transcends any and all of my earthly needs. With Christ my leader and instructor, my trusted counselor, teacher, mediator, and friend, You assure me that I can do everything You ask me to do with the help of the One who gives me the strength to do it *(Philippians 4:13 NLT)*. A living Christ on the inside is more than sufficient to endure all the circumstances on the outside. And so wherever Your finger points me to go, I know You'll make a way. Therefore, I anchor my eternal hope on every Word You promise me ...

1. ***John 3:16, 17 NIV; 17:3 NIV; 10:10; 1 John 4:9,10***
   – You so love the world ... You sent the One most
   precious to You. You gave the One and only gift You
   ever had – Your One and only Son, that I may have
   life, and have it in all its fullness.

2. ***John 6:37 NIV*** – It is Your will and Your sovereignty
   in salvation that You will never, never reject anyone
   who comes to You.

3. ***Psalm 103:8-13*** – Your divine character is that
   You are a Father who pities Your children. You're
   merciful and full of compassion, slow to anger, and
   Your desire is to forgive and bless.

4. ***John 14:18*** – You would never abandon nor leave
   Your children orphaned. Your Holy Spirit will always
   be present to help.

5. ***John 14:12-13*** – When You went to work on the
   building plan of the Kingdom for when Your children would come to live with You, You assured them
   You're coming back to rule, but that they should
   continue the work to do their part and go out into all
   the world and tell others of the Good News of Your
   promise to save those who believe in Jesus Christ
   as Lord and Savior, spreading it abroad to the ends
   of the earth. Everything that Your children need for
   spiritual success has been promised to them. You bid
   them to ask You for whatever they need. But effective prayer is that which is in agreement with Your
   will. And whatever they ask in Jesus' name, You will
   do, so that Your name will be glorified.

6. ***Psalm 34:19*** – Many are the afflictions of the righteous, but You will help us in each and every one
   of them. You will deliver us. For all things work
   together for good to those who love You, to those
   who are called according to Your purpose (*Romans
   8:28-39*).

7. *Hebrews 13:5-6* – Your encouraging promise is that
when I am in dire situations, I should never be in
doubt of Your ability to preserve me, nor should I be
afraid of anyone or anything. For You will never fail
me or forsake me. You will be my helper. My spiritual strength will come from You.

8. *2 Corinthians 12:9* – Every trial becomes a reminder
that Your power rests upon me. When I have painful
thorns in my life, Your grace is sufficient for me. For
when I am weak, I know that I can be strong, and the
less I have the more I can depend on You, my heavenly Father.

9. *John 14:1-4* – You bring comfort to troubled hearts.
You assure me that I should not let anything throw me
into confusion, but instead I should follow through
with my goals by trusting in Your Word. You said
that I should not be insecure, but instead have a future
hope. You said I must not look back, but instead be
forward-looking to attain Your future promise. You
said I must declare the future promise and not the
past disappointments. You said I must press in to get
to my future destiny. Forgetting those things that are
behind, I must lay hold of Christ's purpose for my
life and press on ahead *(Philippians 3:13-14)*, and
live with eager expectation of Your promise and His
return to welcome me into Your Kingdom when He
comes back to rule.

10. *1 John 3:22 KJV* – Your will brings wonderful blessings. All the gifts and blessings that come with Your
salvation have been promised to me. I know I can
come to You and get whatever I ask for, because I
have chosen to obey Your instructions and do what
pleases You.

Chapter

6

Give us this day our daily bread
(Matthew 6:11 KJV)

I Can Learn to Pray
The Lord's Prayer
The Prayer of the Kingdom

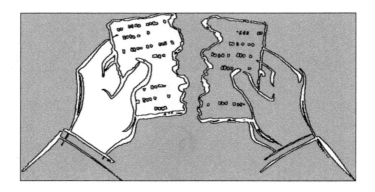

Y ou know what I need. I can't live without it ... I need
whatever it is I need ... whatever I can't live without.
My life is in Your hands, oh Lord; provide for me. When I
don't have whatever I need to live, please make a way for
me. Make a way for me while I leave my old life behind
and follow You to the place where You will bless me *(Genesis
12:1-3 NKJV)* ... while I journey in a strange spiritual land
where I seek Your Kingdom and to align myself with Your
will ... will ... a new land ... the great unknown in which I
don't know yet how to think, how to depend, how to trust,
how to obey, how to pray, or even how to put prayer into
practice. But Father, You said You know all my earthly needs
before I ask You – You know I need the proverbial "bread" to
sustain me, even if, in my lack of spiritual knowledge, I may
not fully grasp that YOU are my Provider ... YOU are the
source of all my supply ... and YOU will supply me "daily."

In Your Word You remind me that *"Man shall not live by
bread alone, but by* EVERY WORD *that proceeds out of Your
mouth (Matthew 4:4; Luke 4:4 KJV).* You tell me that my
earthly needs go beyond bread. You tell me that You are the
source of bread and that You are more important than bread
itself. You instruct me to not only ask for Your provision
but also to align myself with Your will and seek first Your
Kingdom and Your righteousness *(Matthew 6:33),* and then

all these things will be given to me as well, for my source of strength is obedience to Your will.

You said the true Bread is a person, and I must first know You through that person – Your Son, Jesus Christ, my personal Savior and Lord ... The One You sent from heaven *(John 6:33, 35).* Your will is to conform me into Christ's image (the Holy Spirit) of love, joy, peace, patience, kindness, goodness, faithfulness, gentleness, self-control and much more *(Galatians 5:22-23),* so that You can reproduce Your life in me. That's why You want to have a personal and eternal relationship with me through Your plan of salvation.

You sent Christ so that all might be saved from the guilty verdict of sin *(John 3:13-17 NIV; 17:3 NIV)* ... He gives life and light to the world, and Your plan of salvation will preserve all those who believe and put their trust in Him *(John 6:39-40).* He tells me, *"I AM the Bread of Life ... No one who comes to Me will ever be hungry again. Those believing in Me will never thirst"* *(Matthew 4:4; Luke 4:4 KJV; John 6:33, 35; Revelation 7:16-17; 21:6; 22:17).* He tells me, *"Open your heart to the gifts I AM bringing you."* He sets my mind at rest that all that I'm longing for I can have and be blessed. He tells me that I don't have to pay any price to get what He gives *(Isaiah 55:1 KJV),* for the "Bread of Life" He gives is a free gift *(John 6:35)*

My "daily bread" is the personal realization of His presence with me *(Hebrews 13:5)* and His provision *(Hebrews 13:6).* Christ calls this "the Bread of Life." It is nourishment for my soul. It is the only answer to the problem of sin which comes from within. It is the secret of my contentment in every situation *(Philippians 4:12-13 NLT).* When I have this I have all things. Christ said it will help me to develop and possess a spiritual strength that transcends any and all of my earthly needs.

Christ teaches me by word and example always to pray and not lose heart ... always to believe and not doubt His ability to preserve me. His encouraging promise is that He will never leave me nor forsake me *(John 14:18)* ... His relationship with me is such that He is inseparably united with me ... So permanent is this personal, eternal relationship He has established with me, that He will never run off on me ... He will never leave me. He assures me that His grace is sufficient for me *(2 Corinthians 12:9)* and that I must lay hold of His purpose for my life *(Philippians 3:13-14)*, and live with eager expectation of His promise and His return. He assures me that He will always be with me. His presence and provision – the "Bread of Life" – will produce contentment.

Thus You assure me, Father, that when I need help, instead of looking around, I must look up – to You, for You are my helper ... And there's no difficulty too great that You can't fix ... You're the One who made heaven and earth ... You'll send help. You will shelter me from the storm ... for You're my rock ... and my eternal home.

I delight to know Your ways. Your Word has given me understanding *(Proverbs 1:2-7)*. Your instructions have given me hope ... a better way to go ... a better life. My essential nature is to express Your character and to be about "Your business" — expressing Your ideas, witnessing to others about Your nature, sharing what You have taught me through the Lord's Prayer. Your Holy Spirit helps me to realize that when I pray this prayer, I cannot say **"Our"** if I only live for myself. I cannot say **"Father"** if I do not endeavor each day to act like Your child. And, I cannot say **"give us this day our daily bread"** if I ignore the needs of others.

Your Holy Spirit helps me to realize that when I am weak I can be strong, and the less I have the more I can depend on You, my heavenly Father *(2 Corinthians 12:9)*, for every trial reminds me that Your grace is sufficient for me. Thus I can be rich when I'm poor, and I can be generous even in poverty. For Christ and the cross are the source of life

(John 15:5,7 NKJV) ... They give me POWER to go bravely through life no matter what comes.

Because You give me so much wisdom and undeserved kindness, I do not seek in order to just get something from You, but rather to demonstrate sacrificial love to others, bearing one another's burdens, remembering them in their needs by helping them overcome specific difficulties, forgiving them in love and speech and actions which, transcend my human limitations and demonstrate to the world the reality of Christ in me *(Isaiah 58 NKJV; James 1:27)*. Through Christ, I have found that I can help by word and deed, those who cry out for what I and others have taken for granted.

Chapter

7

Forgive us our debts, as we forgive our debtors
(Matthew 6:12 KJV)

I Can Learn to Pray
The Lord's Prayer
The Prayer of the Kingdom

Yอou have not given me the spirit of slavery that would cause me to be afraid of You, nor have You made me one of Your hired servants whereby I am destined to work all my life to pay off my debt to You. Instead, You have adopted me as Your own. And all You have (including all You've achieved) is mine *(Psalm 27:10 NKJV)*. You have given me the spirit of adoption, whereby I call You "Abba" ... Father *(Romans 8:15; Galatians 4:6-7; Ephesians 1:5)*. You have determined to be "my Father" because the law of the Spirit of Life in Christ Jesus has made me FREE from the law of sin and death *(Romans 8:2)*.

I have sinned and broken Your law; therefore I deserve to die. Yet, You have determined to be "my Father" — forgetting all the transgressions I have ever done and remembering them no more. You chose to do this long before I or anyone on earth had yet repented ... long before there was ever any sign of anyone turning towards You. You devised a most remarkable plan in which You would come Yourself, through Christ Your only Son – the living Word – to make peace between the world and Yourself ... restoring the world to Yourself, no longer counting our sins against us, but blotting them out *(2 Corinthians 5:19)*. You sent Your Son – the living Word *(John 1:1 NIV; 1:14 NIV; 1 John 1:1; Revelation 19:13 NKJV)*, to tell us the Good News *(John 3:16-17 NIV; 17:3 NIV)*, what to do *(Acts 2:38-39 NIV)*, and the way to do it *(John 14:6)*.

What a great love You have for an earth filled with people who do not always love You. An earth that rejects You and does not honor You in every way. An earth that knows and understands all that You have done for us, yet does not desire You, nor long for You. In spite of that, what a great love You have lavished on me *(1 John 3:1)*. What a long time You have waited on me. What a great length You have gone to create a pure heart in me ... to put a new and loyal spirit within me ... to make me hate sin ... to lead me to repent ... to make me willing to obey You and to have new delight in Your will *(Psalm 51:1-17)*. Now I know how much You want to take care of me and see my eternal destiny accomplished. Now I know how valuable I am to You. In You I see the fullness of the values I desire.

Therefore, Father, from this day forward, I will uphold Your guiding principles, and I will keep my covenant relationship with You to honor You in every way, and live with the peace and assurance that I am Your child *(Matthew 6:14, 15)*. First, You desire honesty from the heart, so You can teach me to be wise in my inmost being. You said that all sins *must* be confessed to get rid of all my unrighteousness and its consequences *(1 John 1:9)*, and that the correct way of dealing with sin is not to deny it, but to acknowledge it and allow You to cleanse it.

Therefore, I ask You to give me the strength to acknowledge whatever sins that are in my life and confess them to You, knowing that You have already forgiven me, and that

You will never leave me nor forsake me *(John 14:18).* Help me to keep nothing hidden in my heart from You. Please, forgive me for the sins I know about but have trouble overcoming. I confess them to You and I will stop trying to hide them ... instead I will turn away from them ... this is the beginning of the change You have brought about in me. I ask You also to forgive me for the sins I am not aware of, and please help me to become more aware of them. I acknowledge any particular sin I have done and I ask You for continued spiritual growth and cleansing.

Also, You remind me that when I have specifically wronged someone, I must confess the wrongdoing and seek forgiveness from that person *(James 5:16).* All this is done to keep my heart pure. My act of contrition will help to make it much easier for that one who I've wronged to become what he ought to be in You.

Your Kingdom is not about revenge. Your universal law of love and grace works the same for everyone – whether or not they are my enemies. Though I long for the immediate forgiveness and cancellation of my own mistakes and faults, I realize I cannot demand my own release from You if I will not release all those who have ever hurt me. You said I must forgive others and pray for them though they are the ones who need to ask me for forgiveness. Forgiving them is not always easy to do ... I need Your help to do it. For only You can make it possible for me to truly forgive others. But forgiveness is the evidence of a regenerate heart. You desire to free me so that I, despite myself, can speak words of kindness to others and forgive them. That's why, by Your example, You have forgiven me and done a work in my heart. That's why You have given me salvation. That's why I can now forgive and show mercy ... and that's why I can live my life for You. As You show Your goodness to me, so must I show goodness to others.

So, knowing I have a hopeless debt of sin that I owe You, and knowing how undeserving I am, Your graciousness has changed my heart towards others. I thoroughly agree with You that I must forgive them the wrongs they have done me in the same manner that I seek Your forgiveness. Daily You supply my needs and daily You forgive me. Therefore, Father, daily I must forgive others too – I must not hold it against them … no matter who they may be or what they have done. I must come before You with my heart bearing no grudges for anything done to me. For if I don't forgive others, neither will You forgive me.

Chapter

8

Lead us not into temptation
(Matthew 6:13 KJV)

I Can Learn to Pray
The Lord's Prayer
The Prayer of the Kingdom

Iacknowledge how weak I am. Father, protect me from all evil. I live surrounded by temptation, and sometimes I hardly know what to do. But I have learned that I cannot say **"lead us not into temptation"** if I deliberately place myself in its path. So please help me to keep my eyes focused on You. May I never stray from Your will and way, not that I would ever be unfaithful to You. But too many choices to make ... so many lessons to learn ... too much ... too much to face on my own ... It's difficult to resist temptation alone. I desperately need You to help me recognize every evil thing. For if I don't, I'll surely fail! ...If I don't recognize them as evil and stay away from them, I know You'll give me trials to overcome as a way to instruct and admonish me *(James 1:14-15)*.

But You're never the source of temptation, for You don't do wrong and You don't want anyone else to do it *(James 1:13)*. The source of temptation is in me: my own inborn longings, which urge me to yield ... my unrighteousness ... and the enemy of life from outside of me, who pursues me everywhere, offering me "a vice" disguised as "advice." You're never the source of temptation. You will allow temptation in my life so that I may discover what's wrong in me ... that I will wake up!

... and discover Jesus – discover what's right in Him – and find the way out *(John 14:6)*. You will test me in the areas where I need most to grow spiritually so that I may learn to recognize every evil thing. You will test me in order to give me the opportunity to prove my faithfulness to You. You will try my heart and prepare it so that I may have a perfect heart to keep Your commandments; You will change me and leave me emotionally and spiritually better so that my weakness can become my strength and I can reach the eternal destiny You have for me. Meeting Jesus, I suddenly see what I am destined to be.

I can choose my own master and choose sin (with death), or else obedience (with acquittal) and choose You ... I choose You. So I count myself fortunate when You test me with all kinds of difficulties, for I know that when I face such rough times, and I learn life's lessons and patiently receive each entire lesson You intended for me, the result is the ability to endure *(James 1:2-4 NKJV)*. When I face rough times, I know that You'll answer my prayers for help to cope with my trials and temptations by giving me guidance and strength by means of Your Holy Spirit. And Father, I know that whatever You do, You will never let my trials and temptations become greater than what my current level of spiritual understanding can resist and overcome. If I need wisdom to know what You want me to do, all I need to do is ask You, and You will willingly give it to me ... and faith to carry me all the way so that my spiritual eyes will be opened and I can see where I am going.

So help me to remain faithful to succeed in passing the tests and not give in when I'm tempted, that I may receive as Your reward the life You have promised to those who love You *(James 1:12)*. Heaven is the eternal, spiritual destination point for all those who put their trust in You ... Guide my steps all the way to get there *(Psalm 119:133 NLT)* ... Create in me a clean heart filled with clean thoughts and right desires *(Matthew 5:8)*, for You are holy. Let me keep my heart pure, for I want to see You.

Chapter

9

But deliver us from evil
(Matthew 6:13 KJV)

I Can Learn to Pray
The Lord's Prayer
The Prayer of the Kingdom

Father, You have tried my heart and prepared it; You have caused my weakness to become my strength, and I now have a perfect heart to keep Your commandments, yet Satan's snare is more powerful than I can handle. Only You can deliver me. Only You are the solution to every one of Satan's tricks. Only You are the solution to every difficulty. For though You've changed my heart and given me new birth within and I'm growing in grace, still I realize I have an old nature that's capable of sin *(Galatians 5:17)*, I have a sin nature that can once again rule in my heart and life, and I don't want to return to sin. The only way I can be delivered from evil (my old nature) is through the power of Your Holy Spirit– I must constantly look to Christ and the cross *(Romans 6:14; 8:1-2, 11)*, resisting Satan as I remain "steadfast in the faith" *(1Peter 5:9)*, countering every one of his temptations with Your Word, spending time alone with You in prayer at all times, and by doing what is pleasing in Your sight.

With Christ, Your Word which renews my mind, and Your Kingdom in my heart, every trial reminds me that Your grace is sufficient for me. Thus I have found that when I am weak I can be strong, and the less I have the more I can depend on You, my heavenly Father *(2 Corinthians 12:9)*. I have found that through faith in Christ I can be rich when I'm poor, and I can be generous even in poverty. For Christ and the cross are the source of life *(John 15:5, 7 NKJV)* ... They give me POWER to go bravely through life no matter what comes. Therefore, I will not surrender to my circumstances, nor anything which the adversary — the deceiver... the thief ... the enemy of life – may challenge me with. For by Your law of faith *(Hebrews 11:1)*, You have given me AUTHORITY over all things, whereby I can have the assurance of things I hope for as if they were already here, even though I can't actually see them yet.

I will obey with all my heart the teaching to which You have committed me. I will continue to believe in Your truth, for faith is that which persists to the end. Though I do not know where the journey leads, I will leave my old life behind and follow You to the place where You will bless me *(Genesis 12:1-3 NKJV)* ... I will not worry, but instead I will give You thanksgiving and praise in every situation! I will choose to believe Your Word, for I know You're with me. In my moment of crisis I will not let anything throw me into confusion. I will have a future hope. I will declare the future promise and not the past disappointments. I will not look back, but instead I will be forward-looking to attain Your future promise. I will press in to get to my future destiny. Forgetting those things that are behind, I will lay hold of Christ's purpose for my life *(Philippians 3:13-14)*, and live with eager expectation ... of His promise and His return.

Sin dominates the whole world which is under the control of the Evil One. But I am born of God – I will not continue to sin ... For I cannot say, **"Deliver us from evil"** if I'm choosing to participate in doing it. Therefore, by Your grace, deliver me from the evil that awaits me in life. Guide me from sin and help me to avoid temptation instead of having to defeat it. But if I have to fight temptation, help me to not surrender to my circumstances, or anything which the adversary – the deceiver, the thief, the enemy of life – may challenge me with. Keep me safe so that the Evil One cannot touch me *(1 John 5:18)*.

I believe in the name of the Son of God and I know that in Him I have eternal life *(John 3 16-17 NIV; 17:3 NIV)*. You are faithful and true, and my strength and security is in You. By the power of Your Holy Spirit that lives within me I want to do the right thing always, for I stand in the presence of a holy God *(Romans 5:1)*. Manifest the power that You have already put in me, for sin shall not have dominion over me *(Romans 6:14)*. As Christ has overcome, so may I. As Christ was victorious over the power of sin, so I too may walk in this victory by the power of His Holy Spirit which He has given me. For I'm raised up together with Christ! ... I'm being changed to be like Him *(2 Corinthians 3:18)* ... I must live by faith ... I must walk in victory! *(Galatians 3:11; Hebrews 11:1)*. Christ has won the victory and I am complete in Him who is the head of all principality and power. Christ has given me new life through faith in His finished work at the cross. Father, in the name of Jesus, help me to put up a spiritual battle until I gain complete victory over the Evil One. Amen!

Chapter

10

For Thine is the Kingdom, and the power, and the glory, for ever, Amen! *(Matthew 6:13 KJV)*

I Can Learn to Pray

The Lord's Prayer

The Prayer of the Kingdom

Wow! Father, the eternal sovereign **Kingdom** on earth is Yours, the **power** is Yours, and the **glory** is Yours – **forever!** What a victorious end! **AMEN!** – Great Father of heaven and earth, I'm leaping with joy, delight, and praise to You because of Your victory! In six days You created the world and all that ever was and shall be. Yet, You have waited thousands of generations *(Exodus34:6-7)* … until You conquer evil *(Revelation 21:6)*, and set me free from sin and death *(Romans 8:2)*. You have waited thousands of years until I partake of Your perfect righteousness by faith and You win my soul, so that I shall never be separated from You again! You have re-created in me a new nature with disciplined obedience to seek Your glory first … instead of my own. You have re-created in me a new nature to serve and obey You to the very end.

The time You have appointed to forever change the destiny of us all is about to be fulfilled. *"You are worthy, O Lord, to receive glory and honor and power; for You created all things, and by Your will they exist and were created" (Revelation 4:11)*. You are everywhere and in everything, the source of all life and power. Whether it's the glorious demonstration of Your character, strength, ability, and truth, or the quiet beauty with which You display Your peace, patience, truth, justice, mercy, forgiveness, and love, all exist to tell of Your greatness.

I celebrate the gift You have given me, for You have chosen the spiritually poor to be rich in faith and to inherit Your eternal sovereign Kingdom on earth ... to bring us into Your house ... forever! *(Matthew 5:3)* ... You have chosen those who have humbled themselves and acknowledged their sin, and therefore their dependence on You to save them. And because You have redeemed my soul, You have won the victory to claim my heart for You. You're worthy of my adoration. You are Your Majesty, Supreme King, Ultimate Ruler over all the earth, but I can call You "Father." I can boldly enter Your most holy place and talk to You. I can come and talk to You feeling no shame, because my guilty conscience has been washed with Christ's blood to make me clean *(Hebrews 10:19, 21-22)*. When I come into Your presence, You so want Your power and Spirit to flow through me and build up my life *(John 10:10; 15:5,7 NKJV)* that Your kind voice says to me, "Remain in Me," and You promise me, "I will remain in you" *(John 15:4 NKJV)*.

The life-changing prayer You have taught me to pray has changed my heart and has given me new wants and aims. My ardent hope is that You will hear my prayer and that You will bring to pass the highest good in my life ... to know You, and to do Your will. All my petitions to You are my declaration of Your sovereignty and Your right to rule the earth. I come to You through Your only Son, Jesus Christ, whom You have appointed to help me and to show me the way *(John 14:6)*. You not only invite me to make my petitions through Him, but You invite me to have a dwelling place and an assignment to do my part in the heavenly building plan of Your Kingdom on earth, which You have assured me that You're preparing for me *(John 14:2, 23)*. Christ has helped me to know that I must prepare for it as much as You prepare it for me.

You so loved the world and every person You created that when they failed Your test of righteousness *(Genesis 3:13 NKJV)*, You gave Your all to rescue them *(Romans 8:2)*. Because You want to re-create Yourself in me, You have sent Your Word (the Greek word *logos – John 1:1 NIV) –* Your Son Jesus Christ – Your ever-living message to mankind *(John 3:16-17 NIV; 17:3 NIV; 14:6; 18:37)*. Your Word has given me understanding, Your Word has given me hope. Your Word has made me clean. Your Word has conquered sin and death and put new life in me, and my nature has been renewed ... my soul has been redeemed. Your RIGHTEOUSNESS is in me because I have build my house on the RIGHT foundation – Your Son, Jesus Christ, my Savior and Lord. And I thank You for showing me the way to You *(John 3:16-17 NIV; 14:6; 1 Timothy 2:4-6; Matthew 6:9-13 KJV)*.

I have acknowledged my sins and confessed them to You. I have kept nothing hidden in my heart from You. You're so near to me – in my heart ... Your most holy place where You live. Every day I come into Your most holy place and talk to You. Sometimes when I think on Your goodness, knowing how undeserving I am, I just sit there quietly and look up into Your thoughtful loving face. A searching and fearless inventory of what You have done for me runs across my mind ... and I begin to wonder ... where would I be if it wasn't for Your mercy? Where would I be if I had to pay the price for breaking Your law? Thankfully You did ... You took my place and paid the price. Otherwise I would have to fulfill that part for myself – and it would be all over for me ... eternal death would be mine forever! But Your sovereign goodness has saved me from the death penalty – the end result of unforgiven sin.

Your all-knowing eyes can see into my mind and read My thoughts. Even so, Your love and grace answers, "My child, I AM merciful and gracious, and slow to anger. I will not always chastise, neither will I keep My anger forever. I will not deal with you after your sins nor reward you according to your iniquities *(Psalm 103:8-13)*. I do not condemn you *(John 8:11 NIV)*. I care more about your repentance than about what you ever did wrong. I'm happy, not angry to see you return *(Luke 15:23)*. I love you so much, I AM not willing that you should perish *(John 3:16-17 NIV; 17:3 NIV)*. All I know is that once you were lost, but now you're found *(Luke 15:24)*. You will ever be with Me, and all I have is yours. I'm well pleased that you've turned from your wandering ways and chosen new life instead *(John 8:11 NIV)*. Now GO and TELL the Good News to everyone everywhere, of what I've done for you. That anyone who believes in Me will not perish but have everlasting life" *(Matthew 28:18-20; Mark 16:15 NIV; John 3:16 -17 NIV; 17:3 NIV)*.

Father, thank You that even when I struggle to understand every Word You say, I always know that You're so near to me. Your place is so clearly marked. By a step of faith, I've found the way! *(John 3:16-17; 14:6; 1 Timothy 2:4-6; Matthew 6:9-13 KJV)*. And if someone needs to hear about You, by all means, I'll GO and TELL them about You. I'll tell them – *this is what I've seen ... this is what I've heard ... this is what I know about Christ*. I'll tell them about Jesus' death and resurrection, proving Your love for mankind and all that You have done to bring about our redemption *(Acts 1:8 NKJV)*.

Why is it so often the case, dear Father, that for lack of better judgment, the unbeliever contends that Your place is hard to find ... is far away ... or that the road is rocky ... the way is long ... although finding it is just a step of faith outside of his own uncertain world? But Your Kingdom is not far away – it's in our very midst. Your Kingdom is come *(Matthew 6:10)* in our hearts and is yet to come on earth. Your Kingdom is clearly marked because You have shown us the way *(John 1:1 NIV; 3:16-17 NIV; 17:3 NIV; 14:6; 18:37)*. You encourage us to look for it by FAITH, and anyone may find it if they simply ask Your only Son, Jesus Christ, to show them the way. If they do this, they will know with certainty their ultimate destiny. They will know where they are going ... They'll know the way to get there.

To know Christ is to know You, Father. Christ is *the way* – the only way to get to You; He's the embodiment of all *truth*; His is *the perfect life* (of righteousness) You call us to lead *(John 14:6)*. Christ knows what "human" means – that we're not perfect. Otherwise You would not have sent Him to die for us. You would not have sent Him to show us the way. So, for anyone to have a relationship with You as Father, it is only by who Christ is and what He has done for us at the cross. He did not come to perform the function of "religion" but rather to fulfill Your inner spiritual intention – the law of love and grace *(Matthew 5:17,43-48; 7:12; 22:35-40 NLT; John 1:17 NIV; 3:16-17 NIV; 17:3 NIV; 13:34; Romans 7:6; Galatians 3:13; 5:14, 22; Ephesians 2:1, 5, 8, 9; 1 Timothy 1:5; 1 John 3:14)* — which accepts us as we are but cares enough about us to tell us the *truth* about our real condition *(Genesis 2:17; Ezekiel 18:4, 20-24; Romans 3:23; 5:12; 6:23)*, and that You intend to change us and set us free from the predicament of our sinful nature *(Romans 5:12)*. This is the truth Christ brings to all mankind *(John 18:37)*. All You ask is that we *believe*.

Although all have sinned and come short of Your glory *(Romans 3:23)*, and deserve the death penalty *(Romans 6:23)*, Your love has given us an opportunity to find life in the Redeemer – Your Son, Jesus Christ – He is faithful and just to forgive us our sins, and to cleanse us from all unrighteousness *(1 John 1:9).* All we need to do is ask Him to come and rescue us. The eternal importance of this message is tied to the fate of all of our lives. And Your love has the principle that can truly ensure the future for those who will let Christ shape our lives. All that the TRIUMPHANT LIVING LORD has achieved – His redemptive mission which ensures our eternal life – becomes ours if we put our trust in Him and ask Him to forgive our sins and come into our hearts. Christ wants to share this victory and offer this hope to all who trust in Him.

Pontius Pilate asks Christ the haunting question, "What is truth?" *(John 18:38)* ... Philip questions, "Who are You?" *(John 14:8)* ... Pilate insists, "Where do You come from?" *(John 19:9)* ... Peter inquires, "Where are You going?" *(John 14:1-4)* ... Thomas urges, "Show us the way" *(John 14:5-7).* Even as the final event of Christ's life is drawing nearer and there is no time left to contemplate, they still fail to understand His message. And just when it seems the signs were not clearly discerned, the Roman soldier who had thrust the spear into Christ's side, after witnessing all that he has seen, confesses, "Surely He was the Son of God!" *(Matthew 27:54; Mark 15:39).* But alas! This true confession or rather – this declaration of guilt on the part of the Roman Soldier, comes only after he was overcomed with the false suspicion that just another charismatic leader was being crucified, and; only after he in unbelief had joined with those who had falsely judged Christ a condemned sinner worthy of execution ... and they crucified Him *(Matthew 27:35)* ... For thus Satan thought it was to his (Satan's) advantage to prevent everyone from knowing what is the nature of God's love and the redemptive mission of His only Son, Jesus Christ.

But Peter, recognizing Christ for who He is — the triumphant living Lord and the life-giving Savior — shouts with praise to God, "You are the Christ, the Son of the living God!" *(Matthew 16:16)*. Recognizing God's only Son, Nathanael declares, "You are the Son of God, the King of Israel!" *(John 1:49)* And Martha, full of certainty and acceptance of the promise of God, confesses, "I believe You are the Messiah, the Son of God, the One for which the world has so long awaited!" *(John 11:27)*. One and all ... they found that Your Word was true after all.

And as the blood left Christ's body as He hung there on Calvary's cruel cross, every human was given the only way of escaping from the power of sin's slavery. Just as Christ rose again to heaven, in Him the soul re-conquers its sovereignty. Divine justice satisfied the debt of original sin, and that debt was paid for by His sufferings; the bond of man to God was renewed, and thus Christ's death brings life to those who believe. It is the same today as it was then when He rose again to heaven. The voice that carried His tongue and the lips that gave His Holy Spirit wings, even now at this hour ... in a voice loud and clear ... speaks to everyone of us, saying "I AM the resurrection and the life; I AM the One who raises the dead and gives them life again. Anyone who believes in Me will live, even if he dies. He will receive eternal life for believing in Me ... *Do you believe this?"* *(John 11:25-26)*.

The opportunity is clearly given for all to believe ... for all to COME and partake freely *(Psalm 23; Matthew 4:4; 6:33; Luke 4:4 KJV; John 6:33, 35; Romans 3:24; Revelation 7:16-17; 21:6; 22:17)* ... All You ask is that we *believe*. The final event of Your salvation offer is drawing nearer – there's no time left to contemplate. When the last call comes, wherever we are – near or far from You – one and all will find that Your Word was true after all. Everyone can anchor his or her eternal hope on every word Christ has promised, because He is worthy. We can put our trust in Him because only the love of Christ has stood the test of time ... Only the love of Christ can illustrate the extent of what love is through the nature of God's love for every one of us. In actual fact, we can leave our old lives behind and follow Him to the place where You will bless us *(Genesis 12:1-3 NKJV)*, because He is worthy to be believed, for He has triumphed – He has passed all the tests, and in His life, death, and resurrection all the prophecies have met their fulfillment.

Thus we know Father, that we can count on You with our very lives. For You have given us the opportunity to trust You in everything. For in Your Kingdom there is PROVISION, PROTECTION, FORGIVENESS, and now DELIVERANCE – You so loved the world that You gave the One and only gift You ever had ... You gave Your One and only Son, that I may have life, and have it in all its fullness *(John 10:10)*. And to all who receive Him and believe by faith in what He has done for us at the cross and seek Your pardon, they shall have eternal life and not eternal death awaiting them *(John 3:16-17 NIV; 17:3 NIV)* ... to them You shall give the power to become Your children.

And, in spite of all appearances to the contrary, the Lord Jesus reigns in triumph over Satan His enemy! The head that once was crowned with thorns, is crowned with glory now. *"WORTHY IS THE LAMB that was slain!" (Revelation 5:12 NKJV)*. For at the moment of Your eternal victory, You destroyed Satan and his authority over the kingdoms of this world! Yes Jesus, You are the Prince of Peace by virtue of the blood shed on Your cross, for You came armed only with love. You are the Christ — the Son of the LIVING GOD! ... the TRIUMPHANT LIVING LORD! ... the HEAD OF ALL THINGS! ... the FIRSTBORN FROM THE DEAD and of the new creation! ... the POWER OF GOD unto Salvation! ... the One in whom all the fullness of God dwells! ... the EVER EXISTING ONE! The One the world will know and affirm THE VICTOR! The LIGHT OF THE WORLD! ... the One who comes to MAKE ALL THINGS NEW! *(Revelation*

21:5), whose Kingdom is THE BEGINNING OF A NEW ERA IN HUMANKIND when God's home will be on earth among men *(Revelation 21:3)*, when God will ultimately conquer all evil *(Revelation 21:4)*, and all wrongs will be straightened out, all wounds will be healed *(Luke 4:18-19)*, all things incapable of redemption will come to an end, and things will be different tomorrow from what they are like today ... in the New Jerusalem, the Jerusalem of the nations, the Kingdom of justice and peace, the new heaven and earth that You are building, O Lord ... the lasting city where Christ will rule forever. The highest place that heaven has is His by sovereign right.

It is He who holds the FUTURE — the Kingdom on earth — and the reality of that future can be accessible to anyone who will let Him ensure that future for them ... right now *(John 3:16-17 NIV; 17:3 NIV)*, in the name JESUS! – "the Way" *(John 14:6)* ... the road that leads to eternal life. The road that leads to the end of our sins ... the end of eternal separation from God. Everyone has the choice of two roads before them – the road to judgment (eternal death), and the road to Christ (eternal life). The one that leads to Christ will make all the difference! *(John 14:6)*. Our life remains forever undone if we do not take the gift that Christ has so freely given us. But on the other hand, our eternal life begins the moment we say YES to Jesus, and accept His offer of eternal life, which is having a personal relationship with You the true God and Jesus Christ whom You have sent, and living forever in Your presence *(John 17:3 NIV)*. And there's no better time to come and accept that offer than ... right now!

From the moment of Your Son's triumphant victory at Calvary, the earth was compelled to yield to the glory of You, God, our Father, all those who were destined to become Your children. All authority in heaven and on earth has been given to You *(Matthew 28:18)* and none of this will ever change. Somewhere every day someone is deciding, of his own free will, to despise the enemy of life and to choose instead freedom from sin to inherit eternal life in the name of the One You sent, following from the heart the yielding of his or her will to conform to Your will to become Your child, thus bringing Your effective rule on earth.

We see the coming harvest and the fullness of the gentiles coming into faith with You, our Father in heaven *(John 10:16)*. We see You bringing all of Your children together and making us one as You promised *(John 11:52 KJV)*. We see Your vision and Your dream – Your plan of Salvation – the final home-coming of the human family is almost in sight. The time is drawing near. We see You – the Fisherman bringing the fish together in Your net as a hen who gathers her chickens under her wings, and Your promised future expressed in Your love for everyone. Your Kingdom has come ... in our hearts ... in the hearts of all people. The victory is won! You have pulled out the root of sin. The tempter's power is broken. For You have re-created in us a new nature to serve and obey You to the very end! We have seen the light! Your truth has delivered us from the bondage of sin into the freedom of Your eternal sovereign Kingdom which shall bear rule over all the earth, and shall never be destroyed. The glorious light of Your salvation has burst forth into our soul! The seed of Your Word has been planted in our hearts on earth, never to be uprooted, and from which You shall reap a lasting harvest (of souls) for Your Kingdom ... forevermore. Amen!

Therefore, Father, the life of other human beings can no longer be an idle tale, since Your Son JESUS LIVES! Your will is to save all of mankind, and I must hold fast to the proclamation of SALVATION FOR ALL. May I not express condemnation nor be indifferent regarding those who do not yet appear to have been seized by Your Gospel. But help me to gain courage to set myself against the enemy of life – the thief – the lamb-snatcher, and to contest the victory he assumes he has based on the number of prey he has already taken. I must lay hold of CHRIST who is the POWER OF God on earth. His is the power that rescues the lamb that is lost and that has finally won the VICTORY against all powers that are in heaven and on earth. The whole world is destined to become His reward for we can trust Him with our very lives. The glory of His name will come in His being surrounded by countless multitudes – the throng of sheep gathered round the Shepherd's throne … who were scattered in all regions and directions of the earth … all of whom He has wrested from the power of sin and death … will come together safely before His knees *(Philippians 2:10-11)* and His Kingdom stretch from shore to shore. And now as we remain surrounded by Christ's love and guarded by His power, we know that with Him, Father, we hold the "victory" in our hands!

So, let all of Your children say, "Amen! Come quickly Lord Jesus *(Revelation 22:20)*. For our citizenship is with You where You are *(Philippians 3:20)*. As You were taken up to heaven before our very eyes *(Mark 16:19)*, so we live with the eager anticipation of Your return to earth so that You might speak to us face to face again, oh Word of God *(Revelation 19:13 NKJV)*. You will return in judgment and will estab-lish righteousness in the earth" *(Revelation 11:15-17 NKJV; 19:11-16 NKJV)*. When Christ returns, never again will we have to taste the bitter fruit of following an evil course, only to then lose our way again, dear Father. Sin shall tempt us no more. We will be able to contrast the impropriety of sin with the perfection and majesty of Your righteous law. We will not break Your law nor Your loving heart with sin anymore *(Genesis 6:5-6 NLT; Ephesians 4:30)*, but instead we will show willing obedience to Your righteousness. We will be obedient to Your will, fully knowing that man shall not live by bread alone, but by every word that proceeds out of Your mouth *(Matthew 4:4; Luke 4:4 KJV)*.

When You gather the nations and assemble the kingdoms of this world, we shall see evil no more. All enemies, including the spiritual enemy of idolatry that puts others and other things in their lives above You and ignore Your sovereignty, shall be cast out. With disciplined obedience we shall seek Your glory first ... instead of our own. This will result in the universal worship of the only true God, Jehovah *(John 17:3 NIV)*. And everyone will worship You everywhere throughout the world, even in the remotest corners. And You shall reign forevermore! *(Zephaniah 2:11 KJV)*.

Your Word is FAITHFUL and TRUE *(Revelation 19:11 NKJV; 21:5; 22:6)*. Thanks be to You, God our Father, for Your wonderful promise and Your eternal Word. You have made known Your will to us – You desire all to be saved *(1 Timothy 2:4)*, not wishing any to perish *(2 Peter 3:9 NKJV)*. Therefore, I live for the sake of the King and the Kingdom. Everything I do in my life and in my work in the world, I surrender to You, conforming my heart, my mind, and my actions in accordance with Your will, that I may overcome the world *(Revelation 21:7)* as Your only begotten Son Jesus Christ has overcome the world.

As an OVERCOMER, by faith I love, obey, believe, and trust in You and the One You sent *(1 John 5)*. And until Christ comes back to rule, I will bear Your TESTIMONY to the world *(1 John 5:9-12; Revelation 12:11; 17)*, and proclaim its expression through Your EVERLASTING WORD *(Revelation 14:6-7)* until it finds its ultimate expression and release in all creation and Your Kingdom comes on earth in the hearts of all people, and Your will is done. For the strife is over ... the battle is won! The tempter's power is broken. The world now belongs to You, Christ Your Son, and us Your children ... as You intended *(Revelation 11:15 NKJV)* ... and none of this will ever change. And You shall render judgment in every true believer's favor. For they have honored and faithfully served the One You sent. For He is worthy. Worthy is the Lamb ... who sits upon the throne ... who reigns eternally ... who is worthy to be praised *(Revelation 5:1-14 NKJV)*. And under Christ's leadership all nations shall practice justice toward one another. And under His reign, all oppression shall cease. He shall bring love, joy, and peace to all mankind ... and of the increase of HIS GOVERNMENT AND PEACE there shall be no end! *(Isaiah 9:6-7)* ... AMEN.

Index of Bible Quotations

Bible in Basic English (BBE)

King James Version (NKJV)

New King James Version (NKJV)

New Century Version (NCV)

New International Version (NIV)

New Living Translation (NLT)

OLD TESTAMENT

GENESIS

Genesis 1:1 NIV – In the beginning God created the heavens and the earth.

Genesis 1:27-28 – **27** So God created human beings in his image. In the image of God he created them. He created them male and female. **28** God blessed them and said, "Have many children and grow in number. Fill the earth and be its master. Rule over the fish in the sea and over the birds in the sky and over every living thing that moves on the earth."

Genesis 1:31 NKJV – Then God saw everything that He had made, and indeed *it was* very good. So the evening and the morning were the sixth day.

Genesis 2:15-17 – **15** The LORD God put the man in the garden of Eden to care for it and work it. **16** The LORD God commanded him, "You may eat the fruit from any tree in the garden, **17** but you must not eat the fruit from the tree which gives the knowledge of good and evil. If you ever eat fruit from that tree, you will die!"

Genesis 3:1 KJV – Now the serpent was more subtil than any beast of the field which the Lord God had made. And he said unto the woman, Yea, hath God said, Ye shall not eat of every tree of the garden?

Genesis 3:8-9 – **8** Then they heard the LORD God walking in the garden during the cool part of the day, and the man and his wife hid from the LORD God among the trees in the garden. **9** But the LORD God called to the man and said, "Where are you?"

Genesis 3:13 NKJV – And the LORD God said to the woman, "What *is* this you have done?" The woman said, "The serpent deceived me, and I ate."

Genesis 3:15 – I will make you and the woman enemies to each other. Your descendants and her descendants will be enemies. One of her descendants will crush your head, and you will bite his heel.

Genesis 3:17-19 NKJV – **17** Then to Adam He said, "Because you have heeded the voice of your wife, and have eaten from the tree of which I commanded you, saying, 'You shall not eat of it': Cursed *is* the ground for your sake; in toil you shall eat *of* it all the days of your life.

18 Both thorns and thistles it shall bring forth for you, and you shall eat the herb of the field.

19 In the sweat of your face you shall eat bread till you return to the ground, for out of it you were taken; for dust you *are, an*d to dust you shall return."

Genesis 6:5-6 NLT – **5** The Lord observed the extent of human wickedness upon the earth, and he saw that everything they thought or imagined was consistently and totally evil. **6** So the Lord was sorry he had ever made them and put them on earth. It broke his heart.

Genesis 7:1 KJV – And the LORD said unto Noah, Come thou and all thy house into the ark; for thee have I seen righteous before me in this generation.

Genesis 9:20-21 – **20** Noah became a farmer and planted a vineyard. **21** When he drank wine made from his grapes, he became drunk and lay naked in his tent.

Genesis 12:1-3 NKJV – **1** Now the LORD had said to Abram: "Get out of your country, from your family and from your father's house, to a land that I will show you. **2** I will make you a great nation; I will bless you and make your name great; and you shall be a blessing. **3** I will bless those who bless you, and I will curse him who curses you; and in you all the families of the earth shall be blessed."

Genesis 12:13 NKJV – "Please say you *are* my sister, that it may be well with me for your sake, and that I may live because of you."

Genesis 25:29-34 NKJV – **29** Now Jacob cooked a stew; and Esau came in from the field, and he was weary. **30** And Esau said to Jacob, "Please feed me with that same red stew, for I am weary." Therefore his name was called Edom. **31** But Jacob said, "Sell me your birthright as of this day." **32** And Esau said, "Look, I am about to die; so what is this birthright to me?" **33** Then Jacob said, "Swear to me as of this day." So he swore to him, and sold his birthright to Jacob. **34** And Jacob gave Esau bread and stew of lentils; then he ate and drank, arose, and went his way. Thus Esau despised his birthright.

Genesis 27:18-19 NKJV – **18** So he went to his father and said, "My father." And he said, "Here I am. Who *are* you, my son?" **19** Jacob said to his father, "I *am* Esau your firstborn; I have done just as you told me; please arise, sit and eat of my game, that your soul may bless me."

Genesis 48:15 – And Israel blessed Joseph and said, "My ancestors Abraham and Isaac served our God, and like a shepherd God has led me all my life."

EXODUS

Exodus 2:12 NKJV – So he looked this way and that way, and when he saw no one, he killed the Egyptian and hid him in the sand.

Exodus 3:14 NKJV – And God said to Moses, "I AM WHO I AM." And He said, "Thus you shall say to the children of Israel, 'I AM has sent me to you.' "

Exodus 20:1-17 NIV –

The Ten Commandments

1 And God spoke all these words:

2 "I am the LORD your God, who brought you out of Egypt, out of the land of slavery.

3 "You shall have no other gods before me.

4 "You shall not make for yourself an idol in the form of anything in heaven above or on the earth beneath or in the waters below. 5 You shall not bow down to them or worship them; for I, the LORD your God, am a jealous God, punishing the children for the sin of the fathers to the third and fourth generation of those who hate me, 6 but showing love to a thousand {generations} of those who love me and keep my commandments.

7 "You shall not misuse the name of the LORD your God, for the LORD will not hold anyone guiltless who misuses his name.

8 "Remember the Sabbath day by keeping it holy. **9** Six days you shall labor and do all your work, **10** but the seventh day is a Sabbath to the LORD your God. On it you shall not do any work, neither you, nor your son or daughter, nor your manservant or maidservant, nor your animals, nor the alien within your gates. **11** For in six days the LORD made the heavens and the earth, the sea, and all that is in them, but he rested on the seventh day. Therefore the LORD blessed the Sabbath day and made it holy.

12 "Honor your father and your mother, so that you may live long in the land the LORD your God is giving you.

13 "You shall not murder.

14 "You shall not commit adultery.

15 "You shall not steal.

16 "You shall not give false testimony against your neighbor.

17 "You shall not covet your neighbor's house. You shall not covet your neighbor's wife, or his manservant or maidservant, his ox or donkey, or anything that belongs to your neighbor."

Exodus 24:12 KJV – And the LORD said unto Moses, Come up to me into the mount, and be there: and I will give thee tables of stone, and a law, and commandments which I have written; that thou mayest teach them.

Exodus 34:6-7 – **6** The LORD passed in front of Moses and said, "I am the LORD. The LORD is a God who shows mercy, who is kind, who doesn't become angry quickly, who has great love and faithfulness **7** and is kind to thousands of people. The LORD forgives people for evil, for sin, and for turning against him, but he does not forget to punish guilty people. He will punish not only the guilty people, but also their children, their grandchildren, their great-grandchildren, and their great-great-grandchildren."

NUMBERS

Numbers 27:16-17 NIV – **16** May the LORD, the God of the spirits, of all mankind, appoint a man over this community **17** to go out and come in before them, one who will lead them out and bring them in, so the LORD's people will not be like sheep without a Shepherd.

DEUTERONOMY

Deuteronomy 6:6-9 NKJV – **6** "And these words which I command you today shall be in your heart. **7** You shall teach them diligently to your children, and shall talk of them when you sit in your house, when you walk by the way, when you lie down, and when you rise up. **8** You shall bind them as a sign on your hand, and they shall be as frontlets between your eyes. **9** You shall write them on the doorposts of your house and on your gates."

Deuteronomy 6:25 NKJV – Then it will be righteousness for us, if we are careful to observe all these commandments before the LORD our God, as He has commanded us.'

Deuteronomy 7:8 – But the LORD chose you because he loved you, and he kept his promise to your ancestors. So he brought you out of Egypt by his great power and freed you from the land of slavery, from the power of the king of Egypt.

Deuteronomy 16:20 NKJV – You shall follow what is altogether just, that you may live and inherit the land which the LORD your God is giving you.

Deuteronomy 30:15-20 NKJV – **15** "See, I have set before you today life and good, death and evil, **16** in that I command you today to love the LORD your God, to walk in His ways, and to keep His commandments, His statutes, and His judgments, that you may live and multiply; and the LORD your God will bless you in the land which you go to possess. **17** But if your heart turns away so that you do not hear, and are drawn away, and worship other gods and serve them, **18** I announce to you today that you shall surely perish; you shall not prolong *your* days in the land which you cross over the Jordan to go in and possess. **19** I call heaven and earth as witnesses today against you, *that* I have set before you life and death, blessing and cursing; therefore choose life, that both you and your descendants may live; **20** that you may love the LORD your God, that you may obey His voice, and that you may cling to Him, for He *is* your life and the length of your days; and that you may dwell in the land which the LORD swore to your fathers, to Abraham, Isaac, and Jacob, to give them."

Deuteronomy 31:6 NKJV – Be strong and of good courage, do not fear nor be afraid of them; for the LORD your God, He *is* the One who goes with you. He will not leave you nor forsake you."

2 SAMUEL

2 Samuel 11:2-5 NKJV – **2** Then it happened one evening that David arose from his bed and walked on the roof of the king's house. And from the roof he saw a woman bathing, and the woman *was* very beautiful to behold. **3** So David sent and inquired about the woman. And *someone* said, "*Is* this not Bathsheba, the daughter of Eliam, the wife of Uriah the Hittite?"

4 Then David sent messengers, and took her; and she came to him, and he; and she returned to her house. **5** And the woman conceived; so she sent and told David, and said, "I *am* with child."

1 KINGS

1 Kings 19:12-13 NIV – **12** After the earthquake came a fire, but the LORD was not in the fire. After the fire came a gentle whisper. **13** When Elijah heard it, he pulled his cloak over his face and went out and stood at the mouth of the cave. Then a voice said to him, "What are you doing here, Elijah?"

PSALMS

Psalm 2:7 – Now I will tell you what the Lord has declared: He said to me, "You are my son. Today I have become your father."

Psalm 2:9 NKJV – "You shall break them with a rod of iron; You shall dash them to pieces like a potter's vessel."

Psalm 16:10 KJV – For thou wilt not leave my soul in hell; neither wilt thou suffer thine Holy One to see corruption.

Psalm 17:15 – Because I have lived right, I will see your face. When I wake up, I will see your likeness and be satisfied.

Psalm 23

The Lord the Shepherd – A Psalm of David

1 The LORD is my shepherd; I have everything I need. **2** He lets me rest in green pastures. He leads me to calm water. **3** He gives me new strength. He leads me on paths that are right for the good of his name. Even if I walk through a very dark valley, I will not be afraid, because you are with me. **4** Your rod and your shepherd's staff comfort me. **5** You prepare a meal for me in front of my enemies. You pour oil of blessing on my head; you fill my cup to overflowing. **6** Surely your goodness and love will be with me all my life, and I will live in the house of the Lord forever.

Psalm 27:10 NKJV – When my father and my mother forsake me, then the LORD will take care of me.

Psalm 37:29 – Good people will inherit the land and will live in it forever.

Psalm 40:8 – My God, I want to do what you want. Your teachings are in my heart.

Psalm 44:22 NKJV – Yet for Your sake we are killed all day long; we are accounted as sheep for the slaughter.

Psalm 51:1-17

1 God, be merciful to me because you are loving. Because you are always ready to be merciful, wipe out all my wrongs. **2** Wash away all my guilt and make me clean again.

3 I know about my wrongs, and I can't forget my sin. **4** You are the only one I have sinned against; I have done what you say is wrong. You are right when you speak and fair when you judge. **5** I was brought into this world in sin. In sin my mother gave birth to me.

6 You want me to be completely truthful, so teach me wisdom. **7** Take away my sin, and I will be clean. Wash me, and I will be whiter than snow. **8** Make me hear sounds of joy and gladness; let the bones you crushed be happy again. **9** Turn your face from my sins and wipe out all my guilt.

10 Create in me a pure heart, God, and make my spirit right again. **11** Do not send me away from you or take your Holy Spirit away from me. **12** Give me back the joy of your salvation. Keep me strong by giving me a willing spirit. **13** Then I will teach your ways to those who do wrong, and sinners will turn back to you.

14 God, save me from the guilt of murder, God of my salvation, and I will sing about your goodness. **15** Lord, let me speak so I may praise you. **16** You are not pleased by sacrifices, or I would give them. You don't want burnt offerings. **17** The sacrifice God wants is a broken spirit. God, you will not reject a heart that is broken and sorry for sin.

Psalm 87 NLT – **1** On the holy mountain stands the city founded by the Lord. **2** He loves the city of Jerusalem more than any other city in Israel. **3** O city of God, what glorious things are said of you! *(Interlude)*.

4 I will count Egypt and Babylon among those who know me – also Philistia and Tyre, and even distant Ethiopia. They have all become citizens of Jerusalem! **5** Regarding Jerusalem it will be said, "Everyone enjoys the rights of citizenship there." And the Most High will personally bless this city. **6** When the Lord registers the nations, he will say, "They have all become citizens of Jerusalem." *(Interlude).*

7 The people will play flutes and sing, "The source of my life springs from Jerusalem!"

Psalm 95:10 NKJV – For forty years I was grieved with *that* generation, and said, 'It *is* a people who go astray in their hearts, and they do not know My ways.'

Psalm 103:8-14 – 8 The LORD shows mercy and is kind. He does not become angry quickly, and he has great love. 9 He will not always accuse us, and he will not be angry forever. 10 He has not punished us as our sins should be punished; he has not repaid us for the evil we have done. 11 As high as the sky is above the earth, so great is his love for those who respect him. 12 He has taken our sins away from us as far as the east is from west. 13 The LORD has mercy on those who respect him, as a father has mercy on his children. 14 He knows how we were made; He remembers that we are dust.

Psalm 111:10 – Wisdom begins with respect for the Lord; those who obey his orders have good understanding. He should be praised forever.

Psalm 118:6 NKJV – The LORD *is* on my side; I will not fear. What can man do to me?

Psalm 118:22 NKJV – The stone *which* the builders rejected has become the chief cornerstone.

Psalm 119 NLT

The Word of God

Aleph

1 Joyful are people of integrity, who follow the instructions of the LORD. **2** Joyful are those who obey his laws and search for him with all their hearts. **3** They do not compromise with evil, and they walk only in his paths. **4** You have charged us to keep your commandments carefully. **5** Oh, that my actions would consistently reflect your decrees! **6** Then I will not be ashamed when I compare my life with your commands. **7** As I learn your righteous regulations, I will thank you by living as I should! **8** I will obey your decrees. Please don't give up on me!

Beth

9 How can a young person stay pure? By obeying your word. **10** I have tried hard to find you—don't let me wander from your commands. **11** I have hidden your word in my heart, that I might not sin against you. **12** I praise you, O LORD; teach me your decrees. **13** I have recited aloud all the regulations you have given us. **14** I have rejoiced in your laws as much as in riches. **15** I will study your commandments and reflect on your ways. **16** I will delight in your decrees and not forget your word.

Gimel

17 Be good to your servant, that I may live and obey your word. **18** Open my eyes to see the wonderful truths in your instructions. **19** I am only a foreigner in the land. Don't hide your commands from me! **20** I am always overwhelmed with a desire for your regulations. **21** You rebuke the arrogant; those who wander from your commands are cursed. **22** Don't let them scorn and insult me, for I have obeyed your laws. **23** Even princes sit and speak against me, but I will meditate on your decrees. **24** Your laws please me; they give me wise advice.

Daleth

25 I lie in the dust; revive me by your word. **26** I told you my plans, and you answered. Now teach me your decrees. **27** Help me understand the meaning of your commandments, and I will meditate on your wonderful deeds. **28** I weep with sorrow; encourage me by your word. **29** Keep me from lying to myself; give me the privilege of knowing your instructions. **30** I have chosen to be faithful; I have determined to live by your regulations. **31** I cling to your laws. LORD, don't let me be put to shame! **32** I will pursue your commands, for you expand my understanding.

He

33 Teach me your decrees, O LORD; I will keep them to the end. **34** Give me understanding and I will obey your instructions; I will put them into practice with all my heart. **35** Make me walk along the path of your commands, for that is where my happiness is found. **36** Give me an eagerness for your laws rather than a love for money! **37** Turn my eyes from worthless things, and give me life through your word. **38** Reassure me of your promise, made to those who fear you. **39** Help me abandon my shameful ways; for your regulations are good. **40** I long to obey your commandments! Renew my life with your goodness.

Waw

41 LORD, give me your unfailing love, the salvation that you promised me. **42** Then I can answer those who taunt me, for I trust in your word. **43** Do not snatch your word of truth from me, for your regulations are my only hope. **44** I will keep on obeying your instructions forever and ever. **45** I will walk in freedom, for I have devoted myself to your commandments. **46** I will speak to kings about your laws, and I will not be ashamed. **47** How I delight in your commands! How I love them! **48** I honor and love your commands. I meditate on your decrees.

Zayin

49 Remember your promise to me; it is my only hope. **50** Your promise revives me; it comforts me in all my troubles. **51** The proud hold me in utter contempt, but I do not turn away from your instructions. **52** I meditate on your age-old regulations; O LORD, they comfort me. **53** I become furious with the wicked, because they reject your instructions. **54** Your decrees have been the theme of my songs wherever I have lived. **55** I reflect at night on who you are, O LORD; therefore, I obey your instructions. **56** This is how I spend my life: obeying your commandments.

Heth

57 LORD, you are mine! I promise to obey your words! 58 With all my heart I want your blessings. Be merciful as you promised. 59 I pondered the direction of my life, and I turned to follow your laws. 60 I will hurry, without delay, to obey your commands. 61 Evil people try to drag me into sin, but I am firmly anchored to your instructions. 62 I rise at midnight to thank you for your just regulations. 63 I am a friend to anyone who fears you—anyone who obeys your commandments. 64 O LORD, your unfailing love fills the earth; teach me your decrees.

Teth

65 You have done many good things for me, LORD, just as you promised. 66 I believe in your commands; now teach me good judgment and knowledge. 67 I used to wander off until you disciplined me; but now I closely follow your word. 68 You are good and do only good; teach me your decrees. 69 Arrogant people smear me with lies, but in truth I obey your commandments with all my heart. 70 Their hearts are dull and stupid, but I delight in your instructions. 71 My suffering was good for me, for it taught me to pay attention to your decrees. 72 Your instructions are more valuable to me than millions in gold and silver.

Yodh

73 You made me; you created me. Now give me the sense to follow your commands. 74 May all who fear you find in me a cause for joy, for I have put my hope

in your word. **75** I know, O LORD, that your regulations are fair; you disciplined me because I needed it. **76** Now let your unfailing love comfort me, just as you promised me, your servant. **77** Surround me with your tender mercies so I may live, for your instructions are my delight. **78** Bring disgrace upon the arrogant people who lied about me; meanwhile, I will concentrate on your commandments. **79** Let me be united with all who fear you, with those who know your laws. **80** May I be blameless in keeping your decrees; then I will never be ashamed.

Kaph

81 I am worn out waiting for your rescue, but I have put my hope in your word. **82** My eyes are straining to see your promises come true. When will you comfort me? **83** I am shriveled like a wineskin in the smoke, but I have not forgotten to obey your decrees. **84** How long must I wait? When will you punish those who persecute me? **85** These arrogant people who hate your instructions have dug deep pits to trap me. **86** All your commands are trustworthy. Protect me from those who hunt me down without cause. **87** They almost finished me off, but I refused to abandon your commandments. **88** In your unfailing love, spare my life; then I can continue to obey your laws.

Lamedh

89 Your eternal word, O LORD, stands firm in heaven. **90** Your faithfulness extends to every generation, as enduring as the earth you created. **91** Your regulations remain true to this day, for everything serves your plans. **92** If your instructions hadn't sustained me with joy, I would have died in my misery. **93** I will never forget your commandments, for by them you give me life. **94** I am yours; rescue me! For I have worked hard at obeying your commandments. **95** Though the wicked hide along the way to kill me, I will quietly keep my mind on your laws. **96** Even perfection has its limits, but your commands have no limit.

Mem

97 Oh, how I love your instructions! I think about them all day long. **98** Your commands make me wiser than my enemies, for they are my constant guide. **99** Yes, I have more insight than my teachers, for I am always thinking of your laws. **100** I am even wiser than my elders, for I have kept your commandments. **101** I have refused to walk on any evil path, so that I may remain obedient to your word. **102** I haven't turned away from your regulations, for you have taught me well. **103** How sweet your words taste to me; they are sweeter than honey. **104** Your commandments give me understanding; no wonder I hate every false way of life.

Nun

105 Your word is a lamp to guide my feet and a light for my path. **106** I've promised it once, and I'll promise it again: I will obey your righteous regulations. **107** I have suffered much, O LORD; restore my life again as you promised. **108** LORD, accept my offering of praise, and teach me your regulations. **109** My life constantly hangs in the balance, but I will not stop obeying your instructions. **110** The wicked have set their traps for me, but I will not turn from your commandments. **111** Your laws are my treasure; they are my heart's delight. **112** I am determined to keep your decrees to the very end.

Samekh

113 I hate those with divided loyalties, but I love your instructions. **114** You are my refuge and my shield; your word is my source of hope. **115** Get out of my life, you evil-minded people, for I intend to obey the commands of my God. **116** LORD, sustain me as you promised, that I may live! Do not let my hope be crushed. **117** Sustain me, and I will be rescued; then I will meditate continually on your decrees. **118** But you have rejected all who stray from your decrees. They are only fooling themselves. **119** You skim off the wicked of the earth like scum; no wonder I love to obey your laws! **120** I tremble in fear of you; I stand in awe of your regulations.

Ayin

121 Don't leave me to the mercy of my enemies, for I have done what is just and right. **122** Please guarantee a blessing for me. Don't let the arrogant oppress me! **123** My eyes strain to see your rescue, to see the truth of your promise fulfilled. **124** I am your servant; deal with me in unfailing love, and teach me your decrees. **125** Give discernment to me, your servant; then I will understand your laws. **126** LORD, it is time for you to act, for these evil people have violated your instructions. **127** Truly, I love your commands more than gold, even the finest gold. **128**

Each of your commandments is right. That is why I hate every false way.

Pe

129 Your laws are wonderful. No wonder I obey them! **130** The teaching of your word gives light, so even the simple can understand. **131** I pant with expectation, longing for your commands. **132** Come and show me your mercy, as you do for all who love your name. **133** Guide my steps by your word, so I will not be overcome by evil. **134** Ransom me from the oppression of evil people; then I can obey your commandments. **135** Look upon me with love; teach me your decrees. **136** Rivers of tears gush from my eyes because people disobey your instructions.

Tsadhe

137 O LORD, you are righteous, and your regulations are fair. **138** Your laws are perfect and completely trustworthy. **139** I am overwhelmed with indignation, for my enemies have disregarded your words. **140** Your promises have been thoroughly tested; that is why I love them so much. **141** I am insignificant and despised, but I don't forget your commandments. **142** Your justice is eternal, and your instructions are perfectly true. **143** As pressure and stress bear down on me, I find joy in your commands. **144** Your laws are always right; help me to understand them so I may live.

Qoph

145 I pray with all my heart; answer me, LORD! I will obey your decrees. **146** I cry out to you; rescue me, that I may obey your laws. **147** I rise early, before the sun is up; I cry out for help and put my hope in your words. **148** I stay awake through the night, thinking about your promise. **149** In your faithful love, O LORD, hear my cry; let me be revived by following your regulations. **150** Lawless people are coming to attack me; they live far from your instructions. **151** But you are near, O LORD, and all your commands are true. **152** I have known from my earliest days that your laws will last forever.

Resh

153 Look upon my suffering and rescue me, for I have not forgotten your instructions. **154** Argue my case; take my side! Protect my life as you promised. **155** The wicked are far from rescue, for they do not bother with your decrees. **156** LORD, how great is your mercy; let me be revived by following your regulations. **157** Many persecute and trouble me, yet I have not swerved from your laws. **158** Seeing these traitors makes me sick at heart, because they care nothing for your word. **159** See how I love your commandments, LORD. Give back my life because of your unfailing love. **160** The very essence of your words is truth; all your just regulations will stand forever.

Shin

161 Powerful people harass me without cause, but my heart trembles only at your word. **162** I rejoice in your word like one who discovers a great treasure. **163** I hate and abhor all falsehood, but I love your instructions. **164** I will praise you seven times a day because all your regulations are just. **165** Those who love your instructions have great peace and do not stumble. **166** I long for your rescue, LORD, so I have obeyed your commands. **167** I have obeyed your laws, for I love them very much. **168** Yes, I obey your commandments and laws because you know everything I do.

Taw

169 O LORD, listen to my cry; give me the discerning mind you promised. **170** Listen to my prayer; rescue me as you promised. **171** Let praise flow from my lips, for you have taught me your decrees. **172** Let my tongue sing about your word, for all your commands are right. **173** Give me a helping hand, for I have chosen to follow your commandments. **174** O LORD, I have longed for your rescue, and your instructions are my delight. **175** Let me live so I can praise you, and may your regulations help me. **176** I have wandered away like a lost sheep; come and find me, for I have not forgotten your commands.

Psalm 139:1-3 – **1** Lord, You have examined me and know all about me. **2** You know when I sit down and when I get up. You know my thoughts before I think them. **3** You know where I go and where I lie down. You know everything I do.
Psalm 139:14-16 NKJV – **14** I praise you because you made me in an amazing and wonderful way. What you have done is wonderful. I know this very well. **15** My frame was not hidden from You, when I was

made in secret, and skillfully wrought in the lowest parts of the earth. **16** Your eyes saw my substance, being yet unformed. And in Your book they all were written, the days fashioned for me, when as yet there were none of them.

PROVERBS

Proverbs 1:2-7 – **2** They teach wisdom and self-control; they will help you understand wise words. **3** They will teach you how to be wise and self-controlled and will teach you to do what is honest and fair and right. **4** They make the uneducated wise and give knowledge and sense to the young. **5** Wise people can also listen and learn; even they can find good advice in these words. **6** Then anyone can understand wise words and stories, the words of the wise and their riddles. **7** Knowledge begins with respect for the LORD, but fools hate wisdom and discipline. the Lord, but fools hate wisdom and discipline.

Proverbs 23:7 KJV – For as he thinketh in his heart, so is he: Eat and drink, saith he to thee; but his heart is not with thee.

Proverbs 31:8 NIV – Speak up for those who cannot speak for themselves, for the rights of all who are destitute.

ECCLESIASTES

Ecclesiastes 7:20 – Surely there is not a good person on earth who always does good and never sins.

ISAIAH

Isaiah 1:18 KJV – Come now, and let us reason together, saith the LORD: though your sins be as scarlet, they shall be white as snow; though they be red as crimson, they shall be as wool.

Isaiah 2:2-5

2 In the last days the mountain on which the Lord's Temple stands will become the most important of all mountains. t will be raised above the hills, and people from all nations will come streaming to it. **3** Many nations will come and say, "Come, let us go up to the mountain of the LORD, to the Temple of the God of Jacob. Then God will teach us his ways, and we will obey his teachings." His teachings will go out from Jerusalem; the message of the LORD will go out from Jerusalem. **4** He will settle arguments among the nations and will make decisions for many nations. Then they will make their swords into plows and their spears into hooks for trimming trees. Nations will no longer fight other nations, nor will they train for war anymore.

5 Come, family of Jacob, and let us follow the way of the Lord.

Isaiah 7:14 – The Lord himself will give you a sign: The virgin will be pregnant. She will have a son, and she will name him Immanuel.
Isaiah 8:14 NKJV – He will be as a sanctuary, but a stone of stumbling and a rock of offense to both the houses of Israel, as a trap and a snare to the inhabitants of Jerusalem.

Isaiah 9:6-7 – 6 A child has been born to us; God has given a son to us. He will be responsible for leading the people. His name will be Wonderful Counselor, Powerful God, Father Who Lives Forever, Prince of Peace. 7 Power and peace will be in his kingdom and will continue to grow forever. He will rule as king on David's throne and over David's kingdom. He will make it strong by ruling with justice and goodness from now on and forever. The LORD All-Powerful will do this because of his strong love for his people.

Isaiah 11:9 – They will not hurt or destroy each other on all my holy mountain, because the earth will be full of the knowledge of the LORD, as the sea is full of water.

Isaiah 28:16 NKJV – Therefore thus says the Lord GOD: Behold, I lay in Zion a stone for a foundation, a tried stone, a precious cornerstone, a sure foundation; whoever believes will not act hastily.

Isaiah 49:16 NKJV – See, I have written your name on my hand. Jerusalem, I always think about your walls.

Isaiah 50:4-5 –

God's Servant Obeys

4 The Lord GOD gave me the ability to teach so that I know what to say to make the weak strong. Every morning he wakes me. He teaches me to listen like a student. 5 The Lord GOD helps me learn, and I have not turned against him nor stopped following him.

Isaiah 53:6 – We all have wandered away like sheep; each of us has gone his own way. But the

LORD has put on him the punishment for all the evil we have done.

Isaiah 55:1-2 NIV – 1 "Come, all you who are thirsty, come to the waters; and you who have no money, come, buy and eat! Come, buy wind and milk without money and without cost. 2 Why spend money on what is not bread, and your labor on what does not satisfy? Listen, listen to Me, and eat what is good, and your soul will delight in the richest of fare.

Isaiah 55:3 NKJV – Incline your ear, and come to Me. Hear, and your soul shall live; and I will make an everlasting covenant with you— the sure mercies of David.

Isaiah 55:11 – The same thing is true of the words I speak. They will not return to me empty. They make the things happen that I want to happen, and they succeed in doing what I send them to do.

Isaiah 58 NKJV

Fasting That Pleases God

1 "Cry aloud, spare not; lift up your voice like a trumpet; tell My people their transgression, and the house of Jacob their sins. 2 Yet they seek Me daily, and delight to know My ways, as a nation that did righteousness, and did not forsake the ordinance of their God. They ask of Me the ordinances of justice; they take delight in approaching God. 3 'Why have we fasted,' *they say,* 'and You have not seen? Why have we afflicted our souls, and You take no notice?'"

"In fact, in the day of your fast you find pleasure, and exploit all your laborers. 4 Indeed you fast for strife and debate, and to strike with the fist of wickedness. You will not fast as *you do* this day, to make your voice heard on high. **5** Is it a fast that I have chosen, a day for a man to afflict his soul? *Is it* to bow down his head like a bulrush, and to spread out sackcloth and ashes? Would you call this a fast, and an acceptable day to the LORD? **6** "*Is* this not the fast that I have chosen: To loose the bonds of wickedness, to undo the heavy burdens, to let the oppressed go free, and that you break every yoke? **7** *Is it* not to share your bread with the hungry, and that you bring to your house the poor who are cast out; when you see the naked, that you cover him, and not hide yourself from your own flesh? **8** Then your light shall break forth like the morning, your healing shall spring forth speedily, and your righteousness shall go before you; the glory of the LORD shall be your rear guard. **9** Then you shall call, and the LORD will answer; you shall cry, and He will say, 'Here I *am.*'

If you take away the yoke from your midst, the pointing of the finger, and speaking wickedness, **10** *If* you extend your soul to the hungry and satisfy the afflicted soul, then your light shall dawn in the darkness, and your darkness shall *be* as the noonday. **11** The LORD will guide you continually, and satisfy your soul in drought, and strengthen your bones; you shall be like a watered garden, and like a spring of water, whose waters do not fail. **12** Those from among you shall build the old waste places; you shall raise up the foundations of many generations; and you shall be called the Repairer of the Breach, the Restorer of Streets to Dwell In. **13** "If you turn away your foot from the Sabbath, *From* doing your pleasure on My holy day, and call the Sabbath a delight, the holy *day* of the LORD honorable, and shall honor Him, not doing your own ways, nor finding your own pleasure, nor speaking *your own* words, **14** Then you shall delight yourself in the LORD; and I will cause you to ride on the high hills of the earth, and feed you with the heritage of Jacob your father. The mouth of the LORD has spoken."

Isaiah 61:1-2 BBE – 1 The spirit of the Lord GOD is on me, because I am marked out by him to give good news to the poor; he has sent me to make the broken-hearted well, to say that the prisoners will be made free, and that those in chains will see the light again; 2 To give knowledge that the year of the Lord's good pleasure has come, and the day of punishment from our God; to give comfort to all who are sad;

JEREMIAH

Jeremiah 7:23 KJV – But this thing commanded I them, saying, Obey my voice, and I will be your God, and ye shall be my people: and walk ye in all the ways that I have commanded you, that it may be well unto you.

Jeremiah 17:5-13

5 This is what the LORD says: "A curse is placed on those who trust other people, who depend on humans for strength, who have stopped trusting the LORD.6 They are like a bush in a desert that grows in a land where no one lives, a hot and dry land with bad soil. They don't know about the good things God can give.

7 "But the person who trusts in the Lord will be blessed. The Lord will show him that he can be

trusted. **8** He will be strong, like a tree planted near water that sends its roots by a stream. It is not afraid when the days are hot; its leaves are always green. It does not worry in a year when no rain comes; it always produces fruit.

9 "More than anything else, a person's mind is evil and cannot be healed. Who can understand it? **10** But I, the LORD, look into a person's heart and test the mind. So I can decide what each one deserves; I can give each one the right payment for what he does."

11 Like a bird hatching an egg it did not lay, so are the people who get rich by cheating. When their lives are half finished, they will lose their riches. At the end of their lives, it will be clear they were fools.

12 From the beginning, our Temple has been honored as a glorious throne for God. **13** LORD, hope of Israel, those who leave you will be shamed. People who quit following the LORD will be like a name written in the dust, because they have left the LORD, the spring of living water.

Jeremiah 29:11-13 – **11** I say this because I know what I am planning for you," says the LORD. "I have good plans for you, not plans to hurt you. I will give you hope and a good future. **12** Then you will call my name. You will come to me and pray to me, and I will listen to you. **13** You will search for me. And when you search for me with all your heart, you will find me!

Jeremiah 31:33 NKJV – But this *is* the covenant that I will make with the house of Israel after those days, says the LORD: I will put My law in their minds, and write it on their hearts; and I will be their God, and they shall be My people.

EZEKIEL

Ezekiel 18:4 – Every living thing belongs to me. The life of the parent is mine, and the life of the child is mine. The person who sins is the one who will die.

Ezekiel 18:20-24

20 The person who sins is the one who will die. A child will not be punished for a parent's sin, and a parent will not be punished for a child's sin. Those who do right will enjoy the results of their own goodness; evil people will suffer the results of their own evil.

21 "But suppose the wicked stop doing all the sins they have done and obey all my rules and do what is fair and right. Then they will surely live; they will not die. **22** Their sins will be forgotten. Because they have done what is right, they will live. **23** I do not really want the wicked to die, says the Lord GOD. I want them to stop their bad ways and live.

24 "But suppose good people stop doing good and do wrong and do the same hateful things the wicked do. Will they live? All their good acts will be forgotten, because they became unfaithful. They have sinned, so they will die because of their sins.

DANIEL

Daniel 2:44 – During the time of those kings, the God of heaven will set up another kingdom that will never be destroyed or given to another group of people. This kingdom will crush all the other kingdoms and bring them to an end, but it will continue forever.

MICAH

Micah 6:8 KJV – He hath shewed thee, O man, what is good; and what doth the Lord require of thee, but to do justly, and to love mercy, and to walk humbly with thy God?

ZEPHANIAH

Zephaniah 2:11 KJV – The LORD will be terrible unto them: for he will famish all the gods of the earth; and men shall worship him, every one from his place, even all the isles of the heathen.
Zephaniah 3:4 KJV – Her prophets are light and treacherous persons: her priests have polluted the sanctuary, they have done violence to the law.

NEW TESTAMENT

MATTHEW

Matthew 2:2 KJV – Saying, Where is he that is born King of the Jews? for we have seen his star in the east, and are come to worship him.
Matthew 3:11 – I baptize you with water to show that your hearts and lives have changed. But there

is one coming after me who is greater than I am, whose sandals I am not good enough to carry. He will baptize you with the Holy Spirit and fire.

Matthew 4:4 – Jesus answered, "It is written in the Scriptures, 'A person lives not on bread alone, but by everything God says."

Matthew 4:17 – From that time Jesus began to preach, saying, "Change your hearts and lives, because the kingdom of heaven is near."

Matthew 4:23 – Jesus went everywhere in Galilee, teaching in the synagogues, preaching the Good News about the kingdom of heaven, and healing all the people's diseases and sicknesses.

Matthew 5

Jesus Teaches the People

1 When Jesus saw the crowds, he went up on a hill and sat down. His followers came to him, **2** and he began to teach them, saying: **3** "They are blessed who realize their spiritual poverty, for the kingdom of heaven belongs to them. **4** They are blessed who grieve, for God will comfort them. **5** They are blessed who are humble, for the whole earth will be theirs. **6** They are blessed who hunger and thirst after justice, for they will be satisfied. **7** They are blessed who show mercy to others, for God will show mercy to them. **8** They are blessed whose thoughts are pure, for they will see God. **9** They are blessed who work for peace, for they will be called God's children. **10** They are blessed who are persecuted for doing good, for the kingdom of heaven belongs to them.

11 "People will insult you and hurt you. They will lie and say all kinds of evil things about you because you follow me. But when they do, you will be blessed. **12** Rejoice and be glad, because you have a great reward waiting for you in heaven. People did the same evil things to the prophets who lived before you.

You Are Like Salt and Light

13 "You are the salt of the earth. But if the salt loses its salty taste, it cannot be made salty again. It is good for nothing, except to be thrown out and walked on.

14 "You are the light that gives light to the world. A city that is built on a hill cannot be hidden. **15** And people don't hide a light under a bowl. They put it on a lampstand so the light shines for all the people in the house. **16** In the same way, you should be a light for other people. Live so that they will see the good things you do and will praise your Father in heaven.

The Importance of the Law

17 "Don't think that I have come to destroy the law of Moses or the teaching of the prophets. I have not come to destroy them but to bring about what they said. **18** I tell you the truth, nothing will disappear from the law until heaven and earth are gone. Not even the smallest letter or the smallest part of a letter will be lost until everything has happened. **19** Whoever refuses to obey any command and teaches other people not to obey that command will be the least important in the kingdom of heaven. But whoever obeys the commands and teaches other people to obey them will be great in the kingdom of heaven. **20** I tell you that if you are no more obedient than the teachers of the law and the Pharisees, you will never enter the kingdom of heaven.

Jesus Teaches About Anger

21 "You have heard that it was said to our people long ago, 'You must not murder anyone. Anyone who murders another will be judged.' **22** But I tell you, if you are angry with a brother or sister, you will be judged. If you say bad things to a brother or sister, you will be judged by the council. And if you call someone a fool, you will be in danger of the fire of hell.

23 "So when you offer your gift to God at the altar, and you remember that your brother or sister has something against you, **24** leave your gift there at the altar. Go and make peace with that person, and then come and offer your gift.

25 "If your enemy is taking you to court, become friends quickly, before you go to court. Otherwise, your enemy might turn you over to the judge, and the judge might give you to a guard to put you in jail. **26** I tell you the truth, you will not leave there until you have paid everything you owe.

Jesus Teaches About Sexual Sin

27 "You have heard that it was said, 'You must not be guilty of adultery.' **28** But I tell you that if anyone looks at a woman and wants to sin sexually with her, in his mind he has already done that sin with the woman. **29** If your right eye causes you to sin, take it out and throw it away. It is better to lose one part of your body than to have your whole body thrown into hell. **30** If your right hand causes you to sin, cut it off and throw it away. It is better to lose one part of your body than for your whole body to go into hell.

Jesus Teaches About Divorce

31 "It was also said, 'Anyone who divorces his wife must give her a written divorce paper.' **32** But I tell you that anyone who divorces his wife forces her to be guilty of adultery. The only reason for a man to divorce his wife is if she has sexual relations with another man. And anyone who marries that divorced woman is guilty of adultery.

Make Promises Carefully

33 "You have heard that it was said to our people long ago, 'Don't break your promises, but keep the promises you make to the Lord.' **34** But I tell you, never swear an oath. Don't swear an oath using the name of heaven, because heaven is God's throne. **35** Don't swear an oath using the name of the earth, because the earth belongs to God. Don't swear an oath using the name of Jerusalem, because that is the city of the great King. **36** Don't even swear by your own head, because you cannot make one hair on your head become white or black. **37** Say only yes if you mean yes, and no if you mean no. If you say more than yes or no, it is from the Evil One.

Don't Fight Back

38 "You have heard that it was said, 'An eye for an eye, and a tooth for a tooth.' **39** But I tell you, don't stand up against an evil person. If someone slaps you on the right cheek, turn to him the other cheek also. **40** If someone wants to sue you in court and take your shirt, let him have your coat also. **41** If someone forces you to go with him one mile, go with him two miles. **42** If a person asks you for something, give it to him. Don't refuse to give to someone who wants to borrow from you.

Love All People

43 "You have heard that it was said, 'Love your neighbor and hate your enemies.' **44** But I say to you, love your enemies. Pray for those who hurt you. **45** If you do this, you will be true children of your Father in heaven. He causes the sun to rise on good people and on evil people, and he sends rain to those who do right and to those who do wrong. **46** If you love only the people who love you, you will get no reward. Even the tax collectors do that. **47** And if you are nice only to your friends, you are no better than other people. Even those who don't know God are nice to their friends. **48** So you must be perfect, just as your Father in heaven is perfect.

Matthew 6:8 NKJV – Therefore do not be like them. For your Father knows the things you have need of before you ask Him.
Matthew 6:9-13 KJV – **9** After this manner therefore pray ye: Our Father which art in heaven, Hallowed be Thy name. **10** Thy Kingdom come. Thy

will be done in earth, as it is in heaven. **11** Give us this day our daily bread. **12** And forgive us our debts, as we forgive our debtors. **13** And lead us not into temptation, but deliver us from evil: For Thine is the Kingdom, and the power, and the glory, for ever. Amen.

Matthew 6:14-15 – Yes, if you forgive others for their sins, your Father in heaven will also forgive you for your sins. But if you don't forgive others, your Father in heaven will not forgive your sins.

Matthew 6:31-34 NKJV – **31** "Therefore do not worry, saying, 'What shall we eat?' or 'What shall we drink?' or 'What shall we wear?' **32** For after all these things the Gentiles seek. For your heavenly Father knows that you need all these things. *33* Seek first God's kingdom and what God wants. Then all your other needs will be met as well. *34* Therefore do not worry about tomorrow, for tomorrow will worry about itself. Each day has enough trouble of its own.

Matthew 7:12-14

The Most Important Rule

12 Do to others what you want them to do to you. This is the meaning of the law of Moses and the teaching of the prophets.

The Way to Heaven is Hard

13 Enter through the narrow gate. The gate is wide and the road is wide that leads to hell, and many people enter through that gate. **14** But the gate is small and the road is narrow that leads to true life. Only a few people find that road.

Matthew 10:22 – All people will hate you because you follow me, but those people who keep their faith until the end will be saved.

Matthew 10:30 – God even knows how many hairs are on your head.

Matthew 11:28-30 NKJV – **28** "Come to Me, all *you* who labor and are heavy laden, and I will give you rest. **29** Take My yoke upon you and learn from Me, for I am gentle and lowly in heart, and you will find rest for your souls. **30** For My yoke *is* easy and My burden is light."

Matthew 16:13-20

Peter Says Jesus Is the Christ

13 When Jesus came to the area of Caesarea Philippi, he asked his followers, "Who do people say the Son of Man is?"

14 They answered, "Some say you are John the Baptist. Others say you are Elijah, and still others say you are Jeremiah or one of the prophets."

15 Then Jesus asked them, "And who do you say I am?"

16 Simon Peter answered, "You are the Christ, the Son of the living God."

17 Jesus answered, "You are blessed, Simon son of Jonah, because no person taught you that. My Father in heaven showed you who I am. **18** So I tell you, you are Peter. On this rock I will build my church, and the power of death will not be able to defeat it.

19 I will give you the keys of the kingdom of heaven; the things you don't allow on earth will be the things that God does not allow, and the things you allow on earth will be the things that God allows." **20** Then Jesus warned his followers not to tell anyone he was the Christ.

Matthew 18:3-4 – **3** Then he said, "I tell you the truth, you must change and become like little children. Otherwise, you will never enter the kingdom of heaven. **4** The greatest person in the kingdom of heaven is the one who makes himself humble like this child."

Matthew 18:12-14 NKJV – **12** "What do you think? If a man has a hundred sheep, and one of them goes astray, does he not leave the ninety-nine and go to the mountains to seek the one that is straying? **13** And if he should find it, assuredly, I say to you, he rejoices more over that *sheep* than over the ninety-nine that did not go astray. **14** Even so it is not the will of your Father who is in heaven that one of these little ones should own.

Matthew 22:34-40 NLT

The Most Important Commandment

34 But when the Pharisees heard that he had silenced the Sadducees with his reply, they met together to question him again. **35** One of them, an expert in religious law, tried to trap him with this question: **36** "Teacher, which is the most important commandment in the law of Moses?"

37 Jesus replied, "'You must love the LORD your God with all your heart, all your soul, and all your mind.' **38** This is the first and greatest commandment. **39** A second is equally important: 'Love your neighbor as yourself.' **40** The entire law and all the demands of the prophets are based on these two commandments."

Matthew 24:44 NKJV – Therefore you also be ready, for the Son of Man is coming at an hour you do not expect.
Matthew 25:41 NKJV – And anyone not found written in the Book of Life was cast into the lake of fire.

Matthew 26:69-75 NKJV –

Peter Denies Jesus and, Weeps Bitterly

69 Now Peter sat outside in the courtyard. And a servant girl came to him, saying, "You also were with Jesus of Galilee."

70 But he denied it before *them* all, saying, "I do not know what you are saying."

71 And when he had gone out to the gateway, another *girl* saw him and said to those *who were* there, "This *fellow* also was with Jesus of Nazareth."

72 But again he denied with an oath, "I do not know the Man!"

73 And a little later those who stood by came up and said to Peter, "Surely you also are *one* of them, for your speech betrays you."

74 Then he began to curse and swear, *saying,* "I do not know the Man!" Immediately a rooster crowed. **75** And Peter remembered the word of Jesus who had said to him, "Before the rooster crows, you will deny Me three times." So he went out and wept bitterly.

Matthew 27:35 – When the soldiers had cruci-fied him, they threw lots to decide who would get his clothes.

Matthew 27:54 – When the army officer and the soldiers guarding Jesus saw this earthquake and everything else that happened, they were very fright-ened and said, "He really was the Son of God!"

Matthew 28:6-7 NKJV – **6** "He is not here; for He is risen, as He said. Come, see the place where the Lord lay. **7** And go quickly and tell His disci-ples that He is risen from the dead, and indeed He is going before you into Galilee; there you will see Him. Behold, I have told you."

Matthew 28:18-20 – **18** Then Jesus came to them and said, "All power in heaven and on earth is given to me. **19** So go and make followers of all people in the world. Baptize them in the name of the Father and the Son and the Holy Spirit. **20** Teach them to obey everything that I have taught you, and I will be with you always, even until the end of this age."

MARK

Mark 1:17 KJV – And Jesus said unto them, Come ye after me, and I will make you to become fishers of men.

Mark 13:13 – All people will hate you because you follow me, but those people who keep their faith until the end will be saved.

Mark 15:39 – When the army officer who was standing in front of the cross saw what happened when Jesus died, he said, "This man really was the Son of God!"

Mark 16:6 NKJV – But he said to them, "Do not be alarmed. You seek Jesus of Nazareth, who was crucified. He is risen! He is not here. See the place where they laid Him.

Mark 16:11 – But Mary told them that Jesus was alive. She said that she had seen him, but the followers did not believe her.

Mark 16:15-16 NIV – **15** He said to them, "Go into all the world and preach the good news to all creation. **16** Whoever believes and is baptized will be saved, but whoever does not believe will be condemned."

Mark 16:19 NIV – After the Lord Jesus had spoken to them, he was taken up into heaven and he sat at the right hand of God.

LUKE

Luke 2:14 – Give glory to God in heaven, and on earth let there be peace among the people who please God.

Luke 4:4 KJV – And Jesus answered him, saying, It is written, That man shall not live by bread alone, but by every word of God.

Luke 4:18-19 KJV – **18** The Spirit of the Lord is upon me, because he hath anointed me to preach the gospel to the poor; he hath sent me to heal the brokenhearted, to preach deliverance to the captives, and recovery of sight to the blind, to set at liberty them that are bruised,

19 To preach the acceptable year of the Lord.

Luke 9:23 NIV – Then he said to them all: "If anyone would come after me, he must deny himself and take up his cross daily and follow me."

Luke 11:13 NKJV – If you then, being evil, know how to give good gifts to your children, how much more will *your* heavenly Father give the Holy Spirit to those who ask Him!"

Luke 13:3 NIV – I tell you, no! But unless you repent, you too will all perish.

Luke 14:33 KJV – So likewise, whosoever he be of you that forsaketh not all that he hath, he cannot be my disciple.

Luke 15:1-7

The Parable of the Lost Sheep

1 The tax collectors and sinners all came to listen to Jesus. **2** But the Pharisees and the teachers of the law began to complain: "Look, this man welcomes sinners and even eats with them."

3 Then Jesus told them this story: **4** "Suppose one of you has a hundred sheep but loses one of them. Then he will leave the other ninety-nine sheep in the open field and go out and look for the lost sheep until he finds it. **5** And when he finds it, he happily puts it on his shoulders **6** and goes home. He calls to his friends and neighbors and says, 'Be happy with me because I found my lost sheep.' **7** In the same way, I tell you there is more joy in heaven over one sinner who changes his heart and life, than over ninety-nine good people who don't need to change.

Luke 15:11-32

The Parable of the Lost Son

11 Then Jesus said, "A man had two sons. **12** The younger son said to his father, 'Give me my share of the property.' So the father divided the property between his two sons. **13** Then the younger son gathered up all that was his and traveled far away to another country. There he wasted his money in foolish living. **14** After he had spent everything, a time came when there was no food anywhere in the country, and the son was poor and hungry. **15** So he got a job with one of the citizens there who sent the son into the fields to feed pigs. **16** The son was so hungry that he wanted to eat the pods the pigs were eating, but no one gave him anything. **17** When he realized what he was doing, he thought, 'All of my father's servants have plenty of food. But I am here, almost dying with hunger. **18** I will leave and return to my father and say to him, "Father, I have sinned against God and against you. **19** I am no longer worthy to be called your son, but let me be like one of your servants." ' **20** So the son left and went to his father.

"While the son was still a long way off, his father saw him and felt sorry for his son. So the father ran to him and hugged and kissed him. **21** The son said, 'Father, I have sinned against God and against you. I am no longer worthy to be called your son.' **22** But the father said to his servants, 'Hurry! Bring the best clothes and put them on him. Also, put a ring on his finger and sandals on his feet. **23** And get our fat calf and kill it so we can have a feast and celebrate. **24** My son was dead, but now he is alive again! He was lost, but now he is found!' So they began to celebrate.

25 "The older son was in the field, and as he came closer to the house, he heard the sound of music and dancing. **26** So he called to one of the servants and asked what all this meant. **27** The servant said, 'Your brother has come back, and your father killed the fat calf, because your brother came home safely.' **28** The older son was angry and would not go in to the feast. So his father went out and begged him to come in. **29** But the older son said to his father, 'I have served you like a slave for many years and have always obeyed your commands. But you never gave me even a young goat to have at a feast with my friends. **30** But your other son, who wasted all your money on prostitutes, comes home, and you kill the fat calf for him!' **31** The father said to him, 'Son, you are always with me, and all that I have is yours. **32** We had to celebrate and be happy because your brother was dead, but now he is alive. He was lost, but now he is found.' "

Luke 17:20-21 NKJV

The Coming of the Kingdom

20 Now when He was asked by the Pharisees when the kingdom of God would come, He answered them and said, "The kingdom of God does not come with observation; **21** nor will they say, 'See here!' or 'See there!' For indeed, the kingdom of God is within you."

Luke 24:6-7 NKJV – **6** "He is not here, but is risen! Remember how He spoke to you when He was still in Galilee, **7** saying, 'The Son of Man must be delivered into the hands of sinful men, and be crucified, and the third day rise again.'"

Luke 24:23 – But they did not find his body there. They came and told us that they had seen a vision of angels who said that Jesus was alive!

JOHN

John 1:1 NIV –

The Word Became Flesh

In the beginning was the Word, and the Word was with God, and the Word was God.

John 1:12-17 NIV

12 Yet to all who received him, to those who believed in his name, he gave the right to become children of God – **13** children born not of natural decent, nor of human decision or a husband's will, but born of God. **14** The Word became flesh and made his dwelling among us. We have seen his glory, the glory of the One and Only, who came from the Father, full of grace and truth. **15** John testifies concerning him. He cries out, saying, "This was he of whom I said, 'He who comes after me has surpassed me because he was before me.'" **16** From the fullness of his grace we have all received one blessing after another. **17** For the law was given though Moses; grace and truth came through Jesus Christ.

John 1:41 NIV – The first thing Andrew did was to find his brother Simon and tell him, "We have found the Messiah" (that is, the Christ).

John 1:49 – Then Nathanael declared, "Rabbi, you are the Son of God; You are the King of Israel."

John 3 NIV

Jesus Teaches Nicodemus

1 Now there was a man of the Pharisees named Nicodemus, a member of the Jewish ruling council.

2 He came to Jesus at night and said, "Rabbi, we know you are a teacher who has come from God. For no one could perform the miraculous signs you are doing if God were not with him."

3 In reply Jesus declared, "I tell you the truth, no one can see the kingdom of God unless he is born again."

4 "How can a man be born when he is old?" Nicodemus asked. "Surely he cannot enter a second time into his mother's womb to be born!"

5 Jesus answered, "I tell you the truth, no one can enter the kingdom of God unless he is born of water and the Spirit. **6** Flesh gives birth to flesh, but the Spirit gives birth to spirit. **7** You should not be surprised at my saying, 'You must be born again.' **8** The wind blows wherever it pleases. You hear its sound, but you cannot tell where it comes from or where it is going. So it is with everyone born of the Spirit."

9 "How can this be?" Nicodemus asked.

10 "You are Israel's teacher," said Jesus, "and do you not understand these things? **11** I tell you the truth, we speak of what we know, and we testify to what we have seen, but still you people do not accept our testimony. **12** I have spoken to you of earthly things and you do not believe; how then will you believe if I speak of heavenly things? **13** No one has ever gone into heaven except the one who came from heaven— the Son of Man. **14** Just as Moses lifted up the snake in the desert, so the Son of Man must be lifted up, **15** that everyone who believes in him may have eternal life.

16 "For God so loved the world that he gave his one and only Son, that whoever believes in him shall not perish but have eternal life. **17** For God did not send his Son into the world to condemn the world, but to save the world through him. **18** Whoever believes in him is not condemned, but whoever does not believe stands condemned already because he has not believed in the name of God's one and only Son. **19** This is the verdict: Light has come into the world, but men loved darkness instead of light because their deeds were evil. **20** Everyone who does evil hates the light, and will not come into the light for fear that his deeds will be exposed. **21** But whoever lives by the truth comes into the light, so that it may be seen plainly that what he has done has been done through God."

John the Baptist's Testimony About Jesus

22 After this, Jesus and his disciples went out into the Judean countryside, where he spent some time with them, and baptized. **23** Now John also was baptizing at Aenon near Salim, because there was plenty of water, and people were constantly coming to be baptized. **24** (This was before John was put in prison.) **25** An argument developed between some of John's disciples and a certain Jew over the matter of ceremonial washing. **26** They came to John and said to him, "Rabbi, that man who was with you on the other side of the Jordan—the one you testified about—well, he is baptizing, and everyone is going to him."

27 To this John replied, "A man can receive only what is given him from heaven. **28** You yourselves can testify that I said, 'I am not the Christ but am sent ahead of him.' **29** The bride belongs to the bridegroom. The friend who attends the bridegroom waits and listens for him, and is full of joy when he hears the bridegroom's voice. That joy is mine, and it is now complete. **30** He must become greater; I must become less.

31 "The one who comes from above is above all; the one who is from the earth belongs to the earth, and speaks as one from the earth. The one who comes from heaven is above all. **32** He testifies to what he has seen and heard, but no one accepts his testimony. **33** The man who has accepted it has certified that God is truthful. **34** For the one whom God has sent speaks the words of God, for God gives the Spirit without limit. **35** The Father loves the Son and has placed everything in his hands. **36** Whoever believes in the Son has eternal life, but whoever rejects the Son will not see life, for God's wrath remains on him."

John 4:24 – God is spirit, and those who worship him must worship in spirit and truth.

John 6:33 – God's bread is the One who comes down from heaven and gives life to the world.

John 6:35-40 NCV – **35** Then Jesus said, "I am the bread that gives life. Whoever comes to me will never be hungry, and whoever believes in me will never be thirsty." **36** But as I told you before, you have seen me and still don't believe. **37** The Father gives me the people who are mine. Every one of them will come to me, and I will always accept them. **38** I came down from heaven to do what God wants me to do, not what I want to do. **39** Here is what the One who sent me wants me to do: I must not lose even one whom God gave me, but I must raise them all on the last day. **40** Those who see the Son and believe in him have eternal life, and I will raise them on the last day. This is what my Father wants.

John 8:11 NIV – "No one, sir," she said. "Then neither do I condemn you," Jesus declared. "Go now and leave your life of sin."

John 8:31-32

Freedom From Sin

31 So Jesus said to the Jews who believed in him, "If you continue to obey my teaching, you are truly my followers. **32** Then you will know the truth, and the truth will make you free."

John 8:34 – Jesus answered, "I tell you the truth, everyone who lives in sin is a slave to sin."

John 8:36 NIV – So if the Son sets you free, you will be free indeed.

John 9:4-5 NKJV – **4** I must work the works of Him who sent Me while it is day; *the* night is coming when no one can work. **5** As long as I am in the world, I am the light of the world."

John 10:10-18

10 A thief comes to steal and kill and destroy, but I came to give life—life in all its fullness.
11 "I am the good shepherd. The good shepherd gives his life for the sheep. **12** The worker who is paid to keep the sheep is different from the shepherd who owns them. When the worker sees a wolf coming, he runs away and leaves the sheep alone. Then the wolf attacks the sheep and scatters them. **13** The man runs away because he is only a paid worker and does not really care about the sheep.

14 "I am the good shepherd. I know my sheep, and my sheep know me, **15** just as the Father knows me, and I know the Father. I give my life for the sheep. **16** I have other sheep that are not in this flock, and I must bring them also. They will listen to my voice, and there will be one flock and one shepherd. **17** The Father loves me because I give my life so that I can take it back again. **18** No one takes it away from me; I give my own life freely. I have the right to give my life, and I have the right to take it back. This is what my Father commanded me to do."

John 10:27-30 – **27** My sheep listen to my voice; I know them, and they follow me. **28** I give them eternal life, and they will never die, and no one can steal them out of my hand. **29** My Father gave my sheep to me. He is greater than all, and no person can steal my sheep out of my Father's hand. **30** The Father and I are one.

John 11:25-27 – **25** Jesus said to her, "I am the resurrection and the life. Those who believe in me will have life even if they die. **26** And everyone who lives and believes in me will never die. **27** Martha, do you believe this?" Martha answered, "Yes, Lord. I believe that you are the Christ, the Son of God, the One coming to the world."

John 11:52 KJV – And not for that nation only, but that also he should gather together in one the children of God that were scattered abroad.

John 13:34-35 KJV – **34** A new commandment I give unto you, That ye love one another; as I have loved you, that ye also love one another. **35** By this shall all men know that ye are my disciples, if ye have love one to another.

John 14

Jesus Comforts His Disciples

1 Jesus said, "Don't let your hearts be troubled. Trust in God, and trust in me. **2** There are many rooms in my Father's house; I would not tell you this if it were not true. I am going there to prepare a place for you. **3** After I go and prepare a place for you, I will come back and take you to be with me so that you may be where I am. **4** You know the way to the place where I am going."

Jesus as the Way to the Father

5 Thomas said to Jesus, "Lord, we don't know where you are going. So how can we know the way?"

6 Jesus answered, "I am the way, and the truth, and the life. The only way to the Father is through me. **7** If you really knew me, you would know my Father, too. But now you do know him, and you have seen him."

8 Philip said to him, "Lord, show us the Father. That is all we need."

9 Jesus answered, "I have been with you a long time now. Do you still not know me, Philip? Whoever has seen me has seen the Father. So why do you say, 'Show us the Father'? **10** Don't you believe that I am in the Father and the Father is in me? The words I say to you don't come from me, but the Father lives in me and does his own work. **11** Believe me when I say that I am in the Father and the Father is in me. Or believe because of the miracles I have done. **12** I tell you the truth, whoever believes in me will do the same things that I do. Those who believe will do even greater things than these, because I am going to the Father. **13** And if you ask for anything in my name, I will do it for you so that the Father's glory will be shown through the Son. **14** If you ask me for anything in my name, I will do it.

Jesus Promises the Holy Spirit

15 "If you love me, you will obey my commands. **16** I will ask the Father, and he will give you another

Helper to be with you forever **17** — the Spirit of truth. The world cannot accept him, because it does not see him or know him. But you know him, because he lives with you and he will be in you.

18 "I will not leave you all alone like orphans; I will come back to you. **19** In a little while the world will not see me anymore, but you will see me. Because I live, you will live, too. **20** On that day you will know that I am in my Father, and that you are in me and I am in you. **21** Those who know my commands and obey them are the ones who love me, and my Father will love those who love me. I will love them and will show myself to them."

22 Then Judas (not Judas Iscariot) said, "But, Lord, why do you plan to show yourself to us and not to the rest of the world?"

23 Jesus answered, "If people love me, they will obey my teaching. My Father will love them, and we will come to them and make our home with them. **24** Those who do not love me do not obey my teaching. This teaching that you hear is not really mine; it is from my Father, who sent me.

25 "I have told you all these things while I am with you. **26** But the Helper will teach you everything and will cause you to remember all that I told you. This Helper is the Holy Spirit whom the Father will send in my name.

27 "I leave you peace; my peace I give you. I do not give it to you as the world does. So don't let your hearts be troubled or afraid. **28** You heard me say to you, 'I am going, but I am coming back to you.' If you loved me, you should be happy that I am going back to the Father, because he is greater than I am. **29** I have told you this now, before it happens, so that when it happens, you will believe. **30** I will not talk with you much longer, because the ruler of this world is coming. He has no power over me, **31** but the world must know that I love the Father, so I do exactly what the Father told me to do.

"Come now, let us go."

John 15:1-17 NKJV

The True Vine

1 "I am the true vine, and My Father is the vinedresser. **2** Every branch in Me that does not bear fruit He takes away and every *branch* that bears fruit He prunes, that it may bear more fruit. **3** You are already clean because of the word which I have spoken to you. **4** Abide in Me, and I in you. As the branch cannot bear fruit of itself, unless it abides in the vine, neither can you, unless you abide in Me.

5 "I am the vine, you *are* the branches. He who abides in Me, and I in him, bears much fruit; for without Me you can do nothing. **6** If anyone does not abide in Me, he is cast out as a branch and is withered; and they gather them and throw *them* into the fire, and they are burned. **7** If you abide in Me, and My words abide in you, you will ask what you desire, and it shall be done for you. **8** By this My Father is glorified, that you bear much fruit; so you will be My disciples.

Love and Joy Perfected

9 As the Father loved Me, I also have loved you; abide in My love. **10** If you keep My commandments, you will abide in My love, just as I have kept My Father's commandments and abide in His love.

11 "These things I have spoken to you, that My joy may remain in you, and *that* your joy may be full. **12** This is My commandment, that you love one another as I have loved you. **13** Greater love has no one than this, than to lay down one's life for his friends. **14** You are My friends if you do whatever I command you. **15** No longer do I call you servants, for a servant does not know what his master is doing; but I have called you friends, for all things that I heard from My Father I have made known to you. **16** You did not choose Me, but I chose you and appointed you that you should go and bear fruit, and *that* your fruit should remain, that whatever you ask the Father in My name He may give you. **17** These things I command you, that you love one another.

John 15:26 NKJV – "But when the Helper comes, whom I shall send to you from the Father, the Spirit of truth who proceeds from the Father, He will testify of Me."

John 16:1-15

1 "I have told you these things to keep you from giving up. **2** People will put you out of their synagogues. Yes, the time is coming when those who kill you will think they are offering service to God. **3** They will do this because they have not known the

Father and they have not known me. **4** I have told you these things now so that when the time comes you will remember that I warned you.

The Work of the Holy Spirit

"I did not tell you these things at the beginning, because I was with you then. **5** Now I am going back to the One who sent me. But none of you asks me, 'Where are you going? '**6** Your hearts are filled with sadness because I have told you these things. **7** But I tell you the truth, it is better for you that I go away. When I go away, I will send the Helper to you. If I do not go away, the Helper will not come. **8** When the Helper comes, he will prove to the people of the world the truth about sin, about being right with God, and about judgment. **9** He will prove to them that sin is not believing in me. **10** He will prove to them that being right with God comes from my going to the Father and not being seen anymore. **11** And the Helper will prove to them that judgment happened when the ruler of this world was judged.

12 "I have many more things to say to you, but they are too much for you now. **13** But when the Spirit of truth comes, he will lead you into all truth. He will not speak his own words, but he will speak only what he hears, and he will tell you what is to come. **14** The Spirit of truth will bring glory to me, because he will take what I have to say and tell it to you. **15** All that the Father has is mine. That is why I said that the Spirit will take what I have to say and tell it to you.

John 17 NIV

Jesus Prays for Himself

1 After Jesus said this, he looked toward heaven and prayed: "Father, the time has come. Glorify your Son, that your Son may glorify you. **2** For you granted him authority over all people that he might give eternal life to all those you have given him. **3** Now this is eternal life: that they may know you, the only true God, and Jesus Christ, whom you have sent. **4** I have brought you glory on earth by completing the work you gave me to do. **5** And now, Father, glorify me in your presence with the glory I had with you before the world began.

Jesus Prays for His Disciples

6 "I have revealed you to those whom you gave me out of the world. They were yours; you gave them to me and they have obeyed your word. **7** Now they know that everything you have given me comes from you. **8** For I gave them the words you gave me and they accepted them. They knew with certainty that I came from you, and they believed that you sent me. **9** I pray for them. I am not praying for the world, but for those you have given me, for they are yours. **10** All I have is yours, and all you have is mine. And glory has come to me through them. **11** I will remain in the world no longer, but they are still in the world, and I am coming to you. Holy Father, protect them by the power of your name—the name you gave me—so that they may be one as we are one. **12** While I was with them, I protected them and kept them safe by that name you gave me. None has been lost except the one doomed to destruction so that Scripture would be fulfilled. **13** "I am coming to you now, but I say these things while I am still in the world, so that they may have the full measure of my joy within them. I**14** have given them your word and the world has hated them, for they are not of the world any more than I am of the world. **15** My prayer is not that you take them out of the world but that you protect them from the evil one. **16** They are not of the world, even as I am not of it. **17** Sanctify them by the truth; your word is truth. **18** As you sent me into the world, I have sent them into the world. **19** For them I sanctify myself, that they too may be truly sanctified.

Jesus Prays for All Believers

20 "My prayer is not for them alone. I pray also for those who will believe in me through their message, **21** that all of them may be one, Father, just as you are in me and I am in you. May they also be in us so that the world may believe that you have sent me. I**22** have given them the glory that you gave me, that they may be one as we are one: **23** I in them and you in me. May they be brought to complete unity to let the world know that you sent me and have loved them even as you have loved me. **24** "Father, I want those you have given me to be with me where I am, and to see my glory, the glory you have given me because you loved me before the creation of the world. **25** "Righteous Father, though the world does not know you, I know you, and they know that you have sent me. **26** I have made you known to them, and will continue to make you known in order that the love you have for me may be in them and that I myself may be in them."

John 18:36-38

36 Jesus answered, "My kingdom does not belong to this world. If it belonged to this world, my servants would have fought to keep me from being given over to the Jewish leaders. But my kingdom is from another place."

37 Pilate said, "So you are a king!"

Jesus answered, "You are the one saying I am a king. This is why I was born and came into the world: to tell people the truth. And everyone who belongs to the truth listens to me."

38 Pilate said, "What is truth?" After he said this, he went out to the crowd again and said to them, "I find nothing against this man.

John 19:7-9 – **7** The leaders answered, "We have a law that says he should die, because he said he is the Son of God." **9** When Pilate heard this, he was even more afraid. **9** He went back inside the palace and asked Jesus, "Where do you come from?" But Jesus did not answer him.

John 20:8-9 NKJV – **8** Then the other disciple, who came to the tomb first, went in also; and he saw and believed. **9** For as yet they did not know the Scripture, that He must rise again from the dead.

John 20:21-23 – **21** Then Jesus said again, "Peace be with you. As the Father sent me, I now send you." **22** After he said this, he breathed on them and said, "Receive the Holy Spirit. **23** If you forgive anyone his sins, they are forgiven. If you don't forgive them, they are not forgiven."

John 20:31 NKJV – But these are written that you may believe that Jesus is the Christ, the Son of God, and that believing you may have life in His name.

ACTS

Acts 1:3 – After his death, he showed himself to them and proved in many ways that he was alive. The apostles saw Jesus during the forty days after he was raised from the dead, and he spoke to them about the kingdom of God.

Acts 1:4-5 NKJV – **4** And being assembled together with *them,* He commanded them not to depart from Jerusalem, but to wait for the Promise of the Father, "which," *He said,* "you have heard from Me; **5** for John truly baptized with water, but you shall be baptized with the Holy Spirit not many days from now.

Acts 1:8 NKJV – But you shall receive power when the Holy Spirit has come upon you; and you shall be witnesses to Me in Jerusalem, and in all Judea and Samaria, and to the ends of the earth."

Acts 2:1-4 NKJV

Coming of the Holy Spirit

1 When the Day of Pentecost had fully come, they were all with one accord in one place. **2** And suddenly there came a sound from heaven, as of a rushing mighty wind, and it filled the whole house where they were sitting. **3** Then there appeared to them divided tongues, as of fire, and *one* sat upon each of them. **4** And they were all filled with the Holy Spirit and began to speak with other tongues, as the Spirit gave them utterance.

Acts 2:38-39 NIV – 38 Peter replied, "Repent and be baptized, every one of you, in the name of Jesus Christ for the forgiveness of your sins. And you will receive the gift of the Holy Spirit. **39** The promise is for you and your children and for all who are far off – for all whom the Lord our God will call."

Acts 2:42 – They spent their time learning the apostles' teaching, sharing, breaking bread, and praying together.

Acts 2:44-47 NKJV – 44 Now all who believed were together, and had all things in common, **45** and sold their possessions and goods, and divided them among all, as anyone had need.

46 So continuing daily with one accord in the temple, and breaking bread from house to house, they ate their food with gladness and simplicity of heart, **47** praising God and having favor with all the people. And the Lord added to the church daily those who were being saved.

Acts 4:12 – Jesus is the only One who can save people. No one else in the world is able to save us.

Acts 5:12-13 – **12** The apostles did many signs and miracles among the people. And they would all meet together on Solomon's Porch. **13** None of the others dared to join them, but all the people respected them.

Acts 9:6 NKJV – So he, trembling and astonished, said, "Lord, what do You want me to do?" Then the Lord *said* to him, "Arise and go into the city, and you will be told what you must do."

Acts 10:44-48 NKJV

The Holy Spirit Falls on the Gentiles

44 While Peter was still speaking these words, the Holy Spirit fell upon all those who heard the word. **45** And those of the circumcision who believed were astonished, as many as came with Peter, because the gift of the Holy Spirit had been poured out on the Gentiles also. **46** For they heard them speak with tongues and magnify God. Then Peter answered, **47** "Can anyone forbid water, that these should not be baptized who have received the Holy Spirit just as we *have?*" **48** And he commanded them to be baptized in the name of the Lord. Then they asked him to stay a few days.

    Acts 13:29-39 – **29** When they had done to him all that the Scriptures had said, they took him down from the cross and laid him in a tomb. **30** But God raised him up from the dead! **31** After this, for many days, those who had gone with Jesus from Galilee to Jerusalem saw him. They are now his witnesses to the people. **32** We tell you the Good News about the promise God made to our ancestors. **33** God has made this promise come true for us, his children, by raising Jesus from the dead. We read about this also in Psalm 2: 'You are my Son. Today I have become your Father.' *(see Psalm 2:7)*

34 God raised Jesus from the dead, and he will never go back to the grave and become dust. So God said: 'I will give you the holy and sure blessings that I promised to David.' *(see Isaiah 55:3)*

35 But in another place God says: 'You will not let your Holy One rot.' *(see Psalm 16:10)*

36 David did God's will during his lifetime. Then he died and was buried beside his ancestors, and his body did rot in the grave. **37** But the One God raised from the dead did not rot in the grave. **38-39** Brothers, understand what we are telling you: You can have forgiveness of your sins through Jesus. The law of Moses could not free you from your sins. But through Jesus everyone who believes is free from all sins.

Acts 16:29-31 NKJV – **29** Then he called for a light, ran in, and fell down trembling before Paul and Silas. **30** And he brought them out and said, "Sirs, what must I do to be saved?" **31** So they said, "Believe on the Lord Jesus Christ, and you will be saved, you and your household."

Acts 19:1-7

1 While Apollos was in Corinth, Paul was visiting some places on the way to Ephesus. There he found some followers **2** and asked them, "Did you receive the Holy Spirit when you believed?"

They said, "We have never even heard of a Holy Spirit."

3 So he asked, "What kind of baptism did you have?"

They said, "It was the baptism that John taught."

4 Paul said, "John's baptism was a baptism of changed hearts and lives. He told people to believe in the one who would come after him, and that one is Jesus."

5 When they heard this, they were baptized in the name of the Lord Jesus. **6** Then Paul laid his hands on them, and the Holy Spirit came upon them. They began speaking different languages and prophesying. **7** There were about twelve people in this group.

Acts 20:21 – I warned both Jews and Greeks to change their lives and turn to God and believe in our Lord Jesus.

Acts 22:16 – Now, why wait any longer? Get up, be baptized, and wash your sins away, trusting in him to save you.'

Acts 25:19 – The things they said were about their own religion and about a man named Jesus who died. But Paul said that he is still alive.

ROMANS

Romans 3:21-26

Righteousness Through Faith

21 But God has a way to make people right with him without the law, and he has now shown us that way which the law and the prophets told us about. **22** God makes people right with himself through their faith in Jesus Christ. This is true for all who believe in Christ, because all people are the same: **23** Everyone has sinned and fallen short of God's glorious standard, **24** and all need to be made right with God by his grace, which is a free gift. They need to be made free from sin through Jesus Christ. **25** God sent him to die in our place to take away our sins. We receive forgiveness through faith in the blood of Jesus' death. This showed that God always does what is right and

210

fair, as in the past when he was patient and did not punish people for their sins. **26** And God gave Jesus to show today that he does what is right. God did this so he could judge rightly and so he could make right any person who has faith in Jesus.

Romans 4:5 – However, to the man who does not work but trusts God who justifies the wicked, his faith is credited as righteousness.

Romans 5:1-5

Right with God

1 Since we have been made right with God by our faith, we have peace with God. This happened through our Lord Jesus Christ, **2** who through our faith, has brought us into that blessing of God's grace that we now enjoy. And we are happy because of the hope we have of sharing God's glory. **3** We also have joy with our troubles, because we know that these troubles produce patience. **4** And patience produces character, and character produces hope. **5** And this hope will never disappoint us, because God has poured out his love to fill our hearts. He gave us his love through the Holy Spirit, whom God has given to us.

Romans 5:8 – But God demonstrates his own love for us in this: While we were still sinners, Christ died for us.
Romans 5:12 – Sin came into the world because of what one man did, and with sin came death. This is why everyone must die—because everyone sinned.

Romans 6

Dead to Sin but Alive in Christ

1 So do you think we should continue sinning so that God will give us even more grace? **2** No! We died to our old sinful lives, so how can we continue living with sin? **3** Did you forget that all of us became part of Christ when we were baptized? We shared his death in our baptism. **4** When we were baptized, we were buried with Christ and shared his death. So, just as Christ was raised from the dead by the wonderful power of the Father, we also can live a new life.

5 Christ died, and we have been joined with him by dying too. So we will also be joined with him by rising from the dead as he did. **6** We know that our old life died with Christ on the cross so that our sinful selves would have no power over us and we would not be slaves to sin. **7** Anyone who has died is made free from sin's control.

8 If we died with Christ, we know we will also live with him. **1** Christ was raised from the dead, and we know that he cannot die again. Death has no power over him now. **10** Yes, when Christ died, he died to defeat the power of sin one time—enough for all time. He now has a new life, and his new life is with God. **11** In the same way, you should see yourselves as being dead to the power of sin and alive with God through Christ Jesus.

12 So, do not let sin control your life here on earth so that you do what your sinful self wants to do. **13** Do not offer the parts of your body to serve sin, as things

212

to be used in doing evil. Instead, offer yourselves to God as people who have died and now live. Offer the parts of your body to God to be used in doing good. **14** Sin will not be your master, because you are not under law but under God's grace.

Be Slaves of Righteousness

15 So what should we do? Should we sin because we are under grace and not under law? No! **16** Surely you know that when you give yourselves like slaves to obey someone, then you are really slaves of that person. The person you obey is your master. You can follow sin, which brings spiritual death, or you can obey God, which makes you right with him. **17** In the past you were slaves to sin—sin controlled you. But thank God, you fully obeyed the things that you were taught. **18** You were made free from sin, and now you are slaves to goodness. **19** I use this example because this is hard for you to understand. In the past you offered the parts of your body to be slaves to sin and evil; you lived only for evil. In the same way now you must give yourselves to be slaves of goodness. Then you will live only for God.

20 In the past you were slaves to sin, and goodness did not control you. **21** You did evil things, and now you are ashamed of them. Those things only bring death. **22** But now you are free from sin and have become slaves of God. This brings you a life that is only for God, and this gives you life forever. **23** The payment for sin is death. But God gives us the free gift of life forever in Christ Jesus our Lord.

Romans 7:6 -25

6 In the past, the law held us like prisoners, but our old selves died, and we were made free from the law. So now we serve God in a new way with the Spirit, and not in the old way with written rules.

Our Fight Against Sin

7 You might think I am saying that sin and the law are the same thing. That is not true. But the law was the only way I could learn what sin meant. I would never have known what it means to want to take something belonging to someone else if the law had not said, "You must not want to take your neighbor's things." **8** And sin found a way to use that command and cause me to want all kinds of things I should not want. But without the law, sin has no power. **9** I was alive before I knew the law. But when the law's command came to me, then sin began to live, **10** and I died. The command was meant to bring life, but for me it brought death. **11** Sin found a way to fool me by using the command to make me die.

12 So the law is holy, and the command is holy and right and good. **13** Does this mean that something that is good brought death to me? No! Sin used something that is good to bring death to me. This happened so that I could see what sin is really like; the command was used to show that sin is very evil.

The War Within Us

14 We know that the law is spiritual, but I am not spiritual since sin rules me as if I were its slave. **15**

I do not understand the things I do. I do not do what I want to do, and I do the things I hate. **16** And if I do not want to do the hated things I do, that means I agree that the law is good. **17** But I am not really the one who is doing these hated things; it is sin living in me that does them. **18** Yes, I know that nothing good lives in me—I mean nothing good lives in the part of me that is earthly and sinful. I want to do the things that are good, but I do not do them. **19** I do not do the good things I want to do, but I do the bad things I do not want to do. **20** So if I do things I do not want to do, then I am not the one doing them. It is sin living in me that does those things.

21 So I have learned this rule: When I want to do good, evil is there with me. **22** In my mind, I am happy with God's law. **23** But I see another law working in my body, which makes war against the law that my mind accepts. That other law working in my body is the law of sin, and it makes me its prisoner. **24** What a miserable man I am! Who will save me from this body that brings me death? **25** I thank God for saving me through Jesus Christ our Lord!
So in my mind I am a slave to God's law, but in my sinful self I am a slave to the law of sin.

Romans 8

Be Ruled by the Spirit

1 So now, those who are in Christ Jesus are not judged guilty. **2** Through Christ Jesus the law of the Spirit that brings life made you free from the law that brings sin and death. **3** The law was without power, because the law was made weak by our sinful selves. But God did what the law could not do. He sent his own Son to earth with the same human life that others use for sin. By sending his Son to be an offering for sin, God used a human life to destroy sin. **4** He did this so that we could be the kind of people the law correctly wants us to be. Now we do not live following our sinful selves, but we live following the Spirit.

5 Those who live following their sinful selves think only about things that their sinful selves want. But those who live following the Spirit are thinking about the things the Spirit wants them to do. **6** If people's thinking is controlled by the sinful self, there is death. But if their thinking is controlled by the Spirit, there is life and peace. **7** When people's thinking is controlled by the sinful self, they are against God, because they refuse to obey God's law and really are not even able to obey God's law. **8** Those people who are ruled by their sinful selves cannot please God.

9 But you are not ruled by your sinful selves. You are ruled by the Spirit, if that Spirit of God really lives in you. But the person who does not have the Spirit of Christ does not belong to Christ. **10** Your body will always be dead because of sin. But if Christ is in you, then the Spirit gives you life, because Christ made you right with God. **11** God raised Jesus from the dead, and if God's Spirit is living in you, he will also give life to your bodies that die. God is the One who raised Christ from the dead, and he will give life through his Spirit that lives in you.

12 So, my brothers and sisters, we must not be ruled by our sinful selves or live the way our sinful selves want. **13** If you use your lives to do the wrong things your sinful selves want, you will die spiritually. But if you use the Spirit's help to stop doing the wrong things you do with your body, you will have true life.

14 The true children of God are those who let God's Spirit lead them. **15** The Spirit we received does not make us slaves again to fear; it makes us children of God. With that Spirit we cry out, "Father." **16** And the Spirit himself joins with our spirits to say we are God's children. **17** If we are God's children, we will receive blessings from God together with Christ. But we must suffer as Christ suffered so that we will have glory as Christ has glory.

Our Future Glory

18 The sufferings we have now are nothing compared to the great glory that will be shown to us. **19** Everything God made is waiting with excitement for God to show his children's glory completely. **20** Everything God made was changed to become useless, not by its own wish but because God wanted it and because all along there was this hope: **21** that everything God made would be set free from ruin to have the freedom and glory that belong to God's children.

22 We know that everything God made has been waiting until now in pain, like a woman ready to give birth. **23** Not only the world, but we also have been waiting with pain inside us. We have the Spirit as the first part of God's promise. So we are waiting for God to finish making us his own children, which means our bodies will be made free. **24** We were saved, and we have this hope. If we see what we are waiting for, that is not really hope. People do not hope for something they already have. **25** But we are hoping for something we do not have yet, and we are waiting for it patiently.

26 Also, the Spirit helps us with our weakness. We do not know how to pray as we should. But the Spirit himself speaks to God for us, even begs God for us with deep feelings that words cannot explain. **27** God can see what is in people's hearts. And he knows what is in the mind of the Spirit, because the Spirit speaks to God for his people in the way God wants. I consider that our present sufferings are not worth comparing with the glory that will be revealed in us.

More Than Conquerors

28 We know that in everything God works for the good of those who love him. They are the people he called, because that was his plan. **29** God knew them before he made the world, and he chose them to be like his Son so that Jesus would be the firstborn of many brothers and sisters. **30** God planned for them to be like his Son; and those he planned to be like his Son, he also called; and those he called, he also made right with him; and those he made right, he also glorified.

31 So what should we say about this? If God is for us, no one can defeat us. **32** He did not spare his own Son but gave him for us all. So with Jesus, God will surely give us all things. **33** Who can accuse the people God has chosen? No one, because God is the One who makes them right. **34** Who can say God's people are guilty? No one, because Christ Jesus died, but he was also raised from the dead, and now he is on God's right side, appealing to God for us. **35** Can anything separate us from the love Christ has for us? Can troubles or problems or sufferings or hunger or nakedness or danger or violent death? **36** As it is written in the Scriptures: "For you we are in danger of death all the time. People think we are worth no more than sheep to be killed." *(see Psalm 44:22)*

37 But in all these things we are completely victorious through God who showed his love for us. **38** Yes, I am sure that neither death, nor life, nor angels, nor ruling spirits, nothing now, nothing in the future, no powers, **39** nothing above us, nothing below us, nor anything else in the whole world will ever be able to separate us from the love of God that is in Christ Jesus our Lord.

Romans 10:9-15

9 If you declare with your mouth, "Jesus is Lord," and if you believe in your heart that God raised Jesus from the dead, you will be saved. **10** We believe with our hearts, and so we are made right with God. And we declare with our mouths that we believe, and so we are saved. **11** As the Scripture says, "Anyone who trusts in him will never be disappointed." **12** That Scripture says "anyone" because there is no difference between those who are Jews and those who are not. The same Lord is the Lord of all and gives many blessings to all who trust in him, **13** as the Scripture says, "Anyone who calls on the Lord will be saved."

14 But before people can ask the Lord for help, they must believe in him; and before they can believe in him, they must hear about him; and for them to hear about the Lord, someone must tell them; **15** and before someone can go and tell them, that person must be sent. It is written, "How beautiful is the person who comes to bring good news."

Romans 12:1-7 KJV – **1** I beseech you therefore, brethren, by the mercies of God, that ye present your bodies a living sacrifice, holy, acceptable unto God, which is your reasonable service. **2** And be not conformed to this world: but be ye transformed by the renewing of your mind, that ye may prove what is that good, and acceptable, and perfect, will of God **3** For I say, through the grace given unto me, to every man that is among you, not to think of himself more highly than he ought to think; but to think soberly, according as God hath dealt to every man the measure of faith. **4** For as we have many members in one body, and all members have not the same office: **5** So we, being many, are one body in Christ, and every one members one of another. **6** Having then gifts differing according to the grace that is given to us, whether prophecy, let us prophesy according to the proportion of faith; **7** Or ministry, let us wait on our ministering: or he that teacheth, on teaching.

Romans 12:17-21 KJV – **17** Recompense to no man evil for evil. Provide things honest in the sight of all men. **18** If it be possible, as much as lieth in you, live peaceably with all men. **19** Dearly beloved, avenge not yourselves, but rather give place unto wrath: for it is written, Vengeance is mine; I will repay, saith the Lord. – **20** Therefore if thine enemy hunger, feed him; if he thirst, give him drink: for in so doing thou shall heap coals of fire on his head. **21** Be not overcome of evil, but overcome evil with good.

***Romans 13:11-12 KJV* – 11** And that, knowing the time, that now it is high time to awake out of sleep: for now is our salvation nearer than when we believed. **12** The night is far spent, the day is at hand: let us therefore cast off the works of darkness, and let us put on the armour of light.

***Romans 16:20 NKJV* –** And the God of peace will crush Satan under your feet shortly. The grace of our Lord Jesus Christ *be* with you. Amen.

1 CORINTHIANS

1 Corinthians 3:16 NKJV – Do you not know that you are the temple of God and *that* the Spirit of God dwells in you?

1 Corinthians 12:1-12 NKJV

Spiritual Gifts: Unity in Diversity

1 Now concerning spiritual *gifts,* brethren, I do not want you to be ignorant: **2** You know that you were Gentiles, carried away to these dumb idols, however you were led. **3** Therefore I make known to you that no one speaking by the Spirit of God calls Jesus accursed, and no one can say that Jesus is Lord except by the Holy Spirit.**4** There are diversities of gifts, but the same Spirit. **5** There are differences of ministries, but the same Lord. **6** And there are diversities of activities, but it is the same God who works all in all. **7** But the manifestation of the Spirit is given to each one for the profit *of all:* **8** for to one is given the word of wisdom through the Spirit, to another the word of knowledge through the same Spirit, **9** to another faith by the same Spirit, to another gifts of healings by the same Spirit, **10** to another the working of miracles, to another prophecy, to another discerning of spirits, to another *different* kinds of tongues, to another the interpretation of tongues. **11** But one and the same Spirit works all these things, distributing to each one individually as He wills.

Unity and Diversity in One Body

12 For as the body is one and has many members, but all the members of that one body, being many, are one body, so also *is* Christ.

1 Corinthians 12:28 NKJV – And God has appointed these in the church: first apostles, second prophets, third teachers, after that miracles, then gifts of healings, helps, administrations, varieties of tongues.

1 Corinthians 13

Love

1 I may speak in different languages of people or even angels. But if I do not have love, I am only a noisy bell or a crashing cymbal. **2** I may have the gift of prophecy. I may understand all the secret things of God and have all knowledge, and I may have faith so great I can move mountains. But even with all these things, if I do not have love, then I am nothing. **3** I may give away everything I have, and I may even give my body as an offering to be burned. But I gain nothing if I do not have love.

4 Love is patient and kind. Love is not jealous, it does not brag, and it is not proud. **5** Love is not rude, is not selfish, and does not get upset with others. Love does not count up wrongs that have been done. **6** Love takes no pleasure in evil but rejoices over the truth. **7** Love patiently accepts all things. It always trusts, always hopes, and always endures.

8 Love never ends. There are gifts of prophecy, but they will be ended. There are gifts of speaking in different languages, but those gifts will stop. There is the gift of knowledge, but it will come to an end. **9** The reason is that our knowledge and our ability to prophesy are not perfect. **10** But when perfection comes, the things that are not perfect will end. **11** When I was a child, I talked like a child, I thought like a child, I reasoned like a child. When I became a man, I stopped those childish ways. **12** It is the same with us. Now we see a dim reflection, as if we were looking into a mirror, but then we shall see clearly. Now I know only a part, but then I will know fully, as God has known me. **13** So these three things continue forever: faith, hope, and love. And the greatest of these is love.

1 Corinthians 15:1-4 – **1** Now, brothers and sisters, I want you to remember the Good News I brought to you. You received this Good News and continue strong in it. **2** And you are being saved by it if you continue believing what I told you. If you do not, then you believed for nothing. **3** I passed on to you what I received, of which this was most important: that Christ died for our sins, as the Scriptures say; **4** that he was buried and was raised to life on the third day as the Scriptures say.

1 Corinthians 15:24-26 – **24** And then the end will come. At that time Christ will destroy all rulers, authorities, and powers, and he will hand over the kingdom to God the Father. **25** Christ must rule until he puts all enemies under his control. **26** The last enemy to be destroyed will be death. **27** The Scripture says that God put all things under his control. When it says "all things" are under him, it is clear this does not include God himself. God is the One who put everything under his control. **28** After everything has been put under the Son, then he will put himself under God, who had put all things under him. Then God will be the complete ruler over everything.

1 Corinthians 15:34 KJV – Awake to righteousness, and sin not; for some have not the knowledge of God: I speak to your shame.

1 Corinthians 15:58 – So my dear brothers and sisters, stand strong. Do not let anything move you. Always give yourselves fully to the work of the Lord, because you know that your work in the Lord is never wasted.

2 CORINTHIANS

2 Corinthians 3:17-18 – **17** The Lord is the Spirit, and where the Spirit of the Lord is, there is freedom. **18** Our faces, then, are not covered. We all show the Lord's glory, and we are being changed to be like him. This change in us brings ever greater glory, which comes from the Lord, who is the Spirit.

2 Corinthians 5:17-21 **17** If anyone belongs to Christ, there is a new creation. The old things have gone; everything is made new! **18** All this is from God. Through Christ, God made peace between us and himself, and God gave us the work of telling everyone about the peace we can have with him. **19** God was in Christ, making peace between the world and himself. In Christ, God did not hold the world guilty of its sins. And he gave us this message of peace. **20** So we have been sent to speak for Christ. It is as if God is calling to you through us. We speak for Christ when we beg you to be at peace with God. **21** Christ had no sin, but God made him become sin so that in Christ we could become right with God.

2 Corinthians 10:4-5 NKJV – **4** For the weapons of our warfare *are* not carnal but mighty in God for pulling down strongholds, **5** casting down arguments and every high thing that exalts itself against the knowledge of God, bringing every thought into captivity to the obedience of Christ.

2 Corinthians 12:9-10 – **9** But he said to me, "My grace is enough for you. When you are weak, my power is made perfect in you." So I am very happy to brag about my weaknesses. Then Christ's power can live in me. **10** For this reason I am happy when I have weaknesses, insults, hard times, sufferings, and all kinds of troubles for Christ. Because when I am weak, then I am truly strong.

GALATIANS

Galatians 2:20 NKJV – I have been crucified with Christ; it is no longer I who live, but Christ lives in me; and the *life* which I now live in the flesh I live by faith in the Son of God, who loved me and gave Himself for me.

Galatians 3:11 – Now it is clear that no one can be made right with God by the law, because the Scriptures say, "Those who are right with God will live by faith."

Galatians 3:13 – Christ redeemed us from the curse of the law by becoming a curse for us, for it is written: "Cursed is everyone who is hung on a tree."

Galatians 3:19-25 NKJV – **19** What purpose then *does* the law *serve?* It was added because of transgressions, till the Seed should come to whom the promise was made; *and it was* appointed through angels by the hand of a mediator. **20** Now a mediator does not *mediate* for one *only,* but God is one.

21 Is the law then against the promises of God? Certainly not! For if there had been a law given which could have given life, truly righteousness would have been by the law. **22** But the Scripture has confined all under sin, that the promise by faith in Jesus Christ might be given to those who believe. **23** But before faith came, we were kept under guard by the law, kept for the faith which would afterward be revealed. **24** Therefore the law was our tutor *to bring us* to Christ, that we might be justified by faith. **25** But after faith has come, we are no longer under a tutor.

Galatians 4:6-7 – **6** Since you are God's children, God sent the Spirit of his Son into your hearts, and the Spirit cries out, "Father." **7** So now you are not a slave; you are God's child, and God will give you the blessing he promised, because you are his child.

Galatians 5

Freedom in Christ

1 We have freedom now, because Christ made us free. So stand strong. Do not change and go back into the slavery of the law. **2** Listen, I Paul tell you that if you go back to the law by being circumcised, Christ does you no good. **3** Again, I warn every man: If you allow yourselves to be circumcised, you must follow all the law. **4** If you try to be made right with God through the law, your life with Christ is over—you have left God's grace. **5** But we have the true hope that comes from being made right with God, and by the Spirit we wait eagerly for this hope. **6** When we are in Christ Jesus, it is not important if we are circumcised or not. The important thing is faith—the kind of faith that works through love.

7 You were running a good race. Who stopped you from following the true way? **8** This change did not come from the One who chose you. **9** Be careful! "Just a little yeast makes the whole batch of dough rise." **10** But I trust in the Lord that you will not believe those different ideas. Whoever is confusing you with such ideas will be punished.

11 My brothers and sisters, I do not teach that a man must be circumcised. If I teach circumcision, why am I still being attacked? If I still taught circumcision, my preaching about the cross would not be a problem. **12** I wish the people who are bothering you would castrate themselves!

13 My brothers and sisters, God called you to be free, but do not use your freedom as an excuse to do what pleases your sinful self. Serve each other with love. **14** The whole law is made complete in this one command: "Love your neighbor as you love yourself." **15** If you go on hurting each other and tearing each other apart, be careful, or you will completely destroy each other. **Life by the Spirit**

16 So I tell you: Live by following the Spirit. Then you will not do what your sinful selves want. **17** Our sinful selves want what is against the Spirit, and the Spirit wants what is against our sinful selves. The two are against each other, so you cannot do just what you please. **18** But if the Spirit is leading you, you are not under the law.

19 The wrong things the sinful self does are clear: being sexually unfaithful, not being pure, taking part in sexual sins, **20** worshiping gods, doing witchcraft, hating, making trouble, being jealous, being angry, being selfish, making people angry with each other, causing divisions among people, **21** feeling envy, being drunk, having wild and wasteful parties, and doing other things like these. I warn you now as I warned you before: Those who do these things will not inherit God's kingdom. **22** But the Spirit produces the fruit of love, joy, peace, patience, kindness, goodness, faithfulness, **23** gentleness, self-control. There is no law that says these things are wrong. **24** Those who belong to Christ Jesus have crucified their own sinful selves. They have given up their old selfish feelings and the evil things they wanted to do. **25** We get our new life from the Spirit, so we should follow the Spirit. **26** We must not be proud or make trouble with each other or be jealous of each other.

Galatians 6:15-17

Not Circumcision but a New Creation

15 It is not important if a man is circumcised or uncircumcised. The important thing is being the new people God has made. **16** Peace and mercy to those who follow this rule—and to all of God's people.

17 So do not give me any more trouble. I have scars on my body that show I belong to Christ Jesus.

EPHESIANS

Ephesians 1:3-23

Spiritual Blessings in Christ

3 Praise be to the God and Father of our Lord Jesus Christ. In Christ, God has given us every spiritual blessing in the heavenly world. **4** That is, in Christ, he chose us before the world was made so that we would be his holy people—people without blame before him. **5** Because of his love, God had already decided to make us his own children through Jesus Christ. That was what he wanted and what pleased him, **6** and it brings praise to God because of his wonderful grace. God gave that grace to us freely, in Christ, the One he loves. **7** In Christ we are set free by the blood of his death, and so we have forgiveness of sins. How rich is God's grace, **8** which he has given to us so fully and freely. God, with full wisdom and understanding, **9** let us know his secret purpose. This was what God wanted, and he planned to do it through Christ. **10** His goal was to carry out his plan, when the right time came, that all things in heaven and on earth would be joined together in Christ as the head.

Paul's Prayer

11 In Christ we were chosen to be God's people, because from the very beginning God had decided this in keeping with his plan. And he is the One who makes everything agree with what he decides and wants. **12** We are the first people who hoped in Christ, and we were chosen so that we would bring praise to God's glory. **13** So it is with you. When you heard the true teaching—the Good News about your salvation—you believed in Christ. And in Christ, God put his special mark of ownership on you by giving you the Holy Spirit that he had promised. **14** That Holy Spirit is the guarantee that we will receive what God promised for his people until God gives full freedom to those who are his—to bring praise to God's glory.

15 That is why since I heard about your faith in the Lord Jesus and your love for all God's people, **16** I have not stopped giving thanks to God for you. I always remember you in my prayers, **17** asking the God of our Lord Jesus Christ, the glorious Father, to give you a spirit of wisdom and revelation so that you will know him better. **18** I pray also that you will have greater understanding in your heart so you will know the hope to which he has called us and that you will know how rich and glorious are the blessings God has promised his holy people. **19** And you will know that God's power is very great for us who believe. That power is the same as the great strength **20** God used to raise Christ from the dead and put him at his right side in the heavenly world. **21** God has put Christ over all rulers, authorities, powers, and kings, and every title that can be given, not only in this world but also in the next. **22** God put everything under his power and made him the head over everything for the church, **23** which is Christ's body. The church is filled with Christ, and Christ fills everything in every way.

Ephesians 2:1-10

We Now Have Life

1In the past you were spiritually dead because of your sins and the things you did against God. **2** Yes, in the past you lived the way the world lives, following the ruler of the evil powers that are above the earth. That same spirit is now working in those who refuse to obey God. **3** In the past all of us lived like them, trying to please our sinful selves and doing all the things our bodies and minds wanted. We should have suffered God's anger because we were sinful by nature. We were the same as all other people.

4 But God's mercy is great, and he loved us very much. **5** Though we were spiritually dead because of the things we did against God, he gave us new life with Christ. You have been saved by God's grace. **6** And he raised us up with Christ and gave us a seat with him in the heavens. He did this for those in Christ Jesus **7** so that for all future time he could show the very great riches of his grace by being kind to us in Christ Jesus. **8** I mean that you have been saved by grace through believing. You did not save yourselves; it was a gift from God. **9** It was not the result of your own efforts, so you cannot brag about it. **10** God has made us what we are. In Christ Jesus, God made us to do good works, which God planned in advance for us to live our lives doing.

Ephesians 4:1 KJV – I therefore, the prisoner of the Lord, beseech you that ye walk worthy of the vocation wherewith ye are called.
Ephesians 4:11 NKJV – And He Himself gave some *to be* apostles, some prophets, some evangelists, and some pastors and teachers.

Ephesians 4:17-32

The Way You Should Live

17 In the Lord's name, I tell you this. Do not continue living like those who do not believe. Their thoughts are worth nothing. **18** They do not understand, and they know nothing, because they refuse to listen. So they cannot have the life that God gives. **19** They have lost all feeling of shame, and they use their lives for doing evil. They continually want to do all kinds of evil. **20** But what you learned in Christ was not like this. **21** I know that you heard about him, and you are in him, so you were taught the truth that is in Jesus. **1** You were taught to leave your old self—to stop living the evil way you lived before. That old self becomes worse, because people are fooled by the evil things they want to do. **23** But you were taught to be made new in your hearts, **24** to become a new person. That new person is made to be like God—made to be truly good and holy.

25 So you must stop telling lies. Tell each other the truth, because we all belong to each other in the same body. **26** When you are angry, do not sin, and be sure to stop being angry before the end of the day. **27** Do not give the devil a way to defeat you. **28** Those who are stealing must stop stealing and start working. They should earn an honest living for themselves. Then they will have something to share with those who are poor.

29 When you talk, do not say harmful things, but say what people need—words that will help others become stronger. Then what you say will do good to those who listen to you. **30** And do not make the Holy Spirit sad. The Spirit is God's proof that you belong to him. God gave you the Spirit to show that God will make you free when the final day comes. **31** Do not be bitter or angry or mad. Never shout angrily or say things to hurt others. Never do anything evil. **32** Be kind and loving to each other, and forgive each other just as God forgave you in Christ.

Ephesians 5:14 KJV Wherefore he saith, Awake thou that sleepest, and arise from the dead, and Christ shall give thee light.

Ephesians 6:10-24 NKJV

The Whole Armor of God

10 Finally, my brethren, be strong in the Lord and in the power of His might. **11** Put on the whole armor of

God, that you may be able to stand against the wiles of the devil. **12** For we do not wrestle against flesh and blood, but against principalities, against powers, against the rulers of the darkness of this age, against spiritual *hosts* of wickedness in the heavenly *places*. **13** Therefore take up the whole armor of God, that you may be able to withstand in the evil day, and having done all, to stand.

14 Stand therefore, having girded your waist with truth, having put on the breastplate of righteousness, **15** and having shod your feet with the preparation of the gospel of peace; **16** above all, taking the shield of faith with which you will be able to quench all the fiery darts of the wicked one. **17** And take the helmet of salvation, and the sword of the Spirit, which is the word of God; **18** praying always with all prayer and supplication in the Spirit, being watchful to this end with all perseverance and supplication for all the saints—**19** and for me, that utterance may be given to me, that I may open my mouth boldly to make known the mystery of the gospel. **20** for which I am an ambassador in chains; that in it I may speak boldly, as I ought to speak.

A Gracious Greeting

21 But that you also may know my affairs *and* how I am doing, Tychicus, a beloved brother and faithful minister in the Lord, will make all things known to you; **22** whom I have sent to you for this very purpose, that you may know our affairs, and *that* he may comfort your hearts. **23** Peace to the brethren, and love with faith, from God the Father and the

Lord Jesus Christ. **24** Grace *be* with all those who love our Lord Jesus Christ in sincerity. Amen

PHILIPPIANS

Philippians 1:3-11

Paul's Prayer

3 I thank my God every time I remember you, **4** always praying with joy for all of you. **5** I thank God for the help you gave me while I preached the Good News—help you gave from the first day you believed until now. **6** God began doing a good work in you, and I am sure he will continue it until it is finished when Jesus Christ comes again.

7 And I know that I am right to think like this about all of you, because I have you in my heart. All of you share in God's grace with me while I am in prison and while I am defending and proving the truth of the Good News. **8** God knows that I want to see you very much, because I love all of you with the love of Christ Jesus.

9 This is my prayer for you: that your love will grow more and more; that you will have knowledge and understanding with your love; **10** that you will see the difference between good and bad and will choose the good; that you will be pure and without wrong for the coming of Christ; **11** that you will be filled with the good things produced in your life by Christ to bring glory and praise to God.

Philippians 2:5 KJV – Let this mind be in you, which was also in Christ Jesus:

Philippians 2:10-11 – **10** So that every knee will bow to the name of Jesus everyone in heaven, on earth, and under the earth. **11** And everyone will confess that Jesus Christ is Lord and bring glory to God the Father.

Philippians 3:12-21

Continuing Toward Our Goal

12 I do not mean that I am already as God wants me to be. I have not yet reached that goal, but I continue trying to reach it and to make it mine. Christ wants me to do that, which is the reason he made me his. **13** Brothers and sisters, I know that I have not yet reached that goal, but there is one thing I always do. Forgetting the past and straining toward what is ahead, **14** I keep trying to reach the goal and get the prize for which God called me through Christ to the life above.

15 All of us who are spiritually mature should think this way, too. And if there are things you do not agree with, God will make them clear to you. **16** But we should continue following the truth we already have.

17 Brothers and sisters, all of you should try to follow my example and to copy those who live the way we showed you. **18** Many people live like enemies of the cross of Christ. I have often told you about them, and it makes me cry to tell you about them now. **19** In the end, they will be destroyed. They do whatever their bodies want, they are proud of their shameful acts, and they think only about earthly things. **20** But our homeland is in heaven, and we are waiting for our Savior, the Lord Jesus Christ, to come from heaven. **21** By his power to rule all things, he will change our humble bodies and make them like his own glorious body.

Philippians 4:12-13 NLT – **12** I know how to live on almost nothing or with everything. I have learned the secret of living in every situation, whether it is with a full stomach or empty, with plenty or little. **13** For I can do everything through Christ, who gives me strength.

COLOSSIANS

Colossians 3:1-17

Your New Life in Christ

1 Since you were raised from the dead with Christ, aim at what is in heaven, where Christ is sitting at the right hand of God. **2** Think only about the things in heaven, not the things on earth. **3** Your old sinful self has died, and your new life is kept with Christ in God. **4** Christ is your life, and when he comes again, you will share in his glory.

5 So put all evil things out of your life: sexual sinning, doing evil, letting evil thoughts control you, wanting things that are evil, and greed. This is really serving a false god. **6** These things make God angry. **7** In your past, evil life you also did these things.

8 But now also put these things out of your life: anger, bad temper, doing or saying things to hurt others, and using evil words when you talk. **9** Do not lie to each other. You have left your old sinful life and the things you did before. **10** You have begun to live the new life, in which you are being made new and are becoming like the One who made you. This new life brings you the true knowledge of God. **11** In the new life there is no difference between Greeks and Jews, those who are circumcised and those who are not circumcised, or people who are foreigners, or Scythians. There is no difference between slaves and free people. But Christ is in all believers, and Christ is all that is important.

12 God has chosen you and made you his holy people. He loves you. So you should always clothe yourselves with mercy, kindness, humility, gentleness, and patience. **13** Bear with each other, and forgive each other. If someone does wrong to you, forgive that person because the Lord forgave you. **14** Even more than all this, clothe yourself in love. Love is what holds you all together in perfect unity. **15** Let the peace that Christ gives control your thinking, because you were all called together in one body to have peace. Always be thankful. **16** Let the teaching of Christ live in you richly. Use all wisdom to teach and instruct each other by singing psalms, hymns, and spiritual songs with thankfulness in your hearts to God. **17** Everything you do or say should be done to obey Jesus your Lord. And in all you do, give thanks to God the Father through Jesus.

2 THESSALONIANS

2 Thessalonians 2:15 NKJV

Stand Fast

Therefore, brethren, stand fast and hold the traditions which you were taught, whether by word or our epistle.

1 TIMOTHY

1 Timothy 1:5 – The purpose of this command is for people to have love, a love that comes from a pure heart and a good conscience and a true faith.

1 Timothy 2:4-6 – 4 Who wants all people to be saved and to know the truth. 5 There is one God and one mediator so that human beings can reach God. That way is through Christ Jesus, who is himself human. 6 He gave himself as a payment to free all people. He is proof that came at the right time.

2 TIMOTHY

2 Timothy 3:14 – But you should continue following the teachings you learned. You know they are true, because you trust those who taught you.

2 Timothy 4:7 NKJV – I have fought the good fight, I have finished the race, I have kept the faith.

TITUS

Titus 2:14 KJV – Who gave himself for us, that he might redeem us from all iniquity, and purify unto himself a peculiar people, zealous of good works.

HEBREWS

Hebrews 1:1-3 NKJV

God's Supreme Revelation

1 God, who at various times and in various ways spoke in time past to the fathers by the prophets, **2** has in these last days spoken to us by *His* Son, whom He has appointed heir of all things, through whom also He made the worlds; **3** who being the brightness of *His* glory and the express image of His person, and upholding all things by the word of His power, when He had by Himself purged our sins, sat down at the right hand of the Majesty on high, **4** having become so much better than the angels, as He has by inheritance obtained a more excellent name than they.

Hebrews 3:15 KJV – While it is said, To day if ye will hear his voice, harden not your hearts, as in the provocation.

Hebrews 7:18-19 NKJV – **18** For on the one hand there is an annulling of the former commandment because of its weakness and unprofitableness, **19** for the law made nothing perfect; on the other hand, there is the bringing in of a better hope, through which we draw near to God.

Hebrews 8:6-8 NLT – **6** But now Jesus, our High Priest, has been given a ministry that is far superior to the old priesthood, for he is the one who mediates for us a far better covenant with God, based on better promises.

7 If the first covenant had been faultless, there would have been no need for a second covenant to replace it. **8** But when God found fault with the people, he said: "The day is coming, says the LORD, when I will make a new covenant with the people of Israel and Judah.

Hebrews 10:19-22 – **19** So, brothers and sisters, we are completely free to enter the Most Holy Place without fear because of the blood of Jesus' death. **20** We can enter through a new and living way that Jesus opened for us. It leads through the curtain—Christ's body. **22** And since we have a great priest over God's house, **21** let us come near to God with a sincere heart and a sure faith, because we have been made free from a guilty conscience, and our bodies have been washed with pure water.

Hebrews 10:25 – You should not stay away from the church meetings, as some are doing, but you should meet together and encourage each other. Do this even more as you see the day coming.

Hebrews 11:1-40

What is Faith?

1 Faith means being sure of the things we hope for and knowing that something is real even if we do not see it. **2** Faith is the reason we remember great people who lived in the past.

3 It is by faith we understand that the whole world was made by God's command so what we see was made by something that cannot be seen.

4 It was by faith that Abel offered God a better sacrifice than Cain did. God said he was pleased with the gifts Abel offered and called Abel a good man because of his faith. Abel died, but through his faith he is still speaking.

5 It was by faith that Enoch was taken to heaven so he would not die. He could not be found, because God had taken him away. Before he was taken, the Scripture says that he was a man who truly pleased God. **6** Without faith no one can please God. Anyone who comes to God must believe that he is real and that he rewards those who truly want to find him.

7 It was by faith that Noah heard God's warnings about things he could not yet see. He obeyed God and built a large boat to save his family. By his faith, Noah showed that the world was wrong, and he became one of those who are made right with God through faith.

8 It was by faith Abraham obeyed God's call to go to another place God promised to give him. He left his own country, not knowing where he was to go. **9** It was by faith that he lived like a foreigner in the country God promised to give him. He lived in tents with Isaac and Jacob, who had received that same promise from God. **10** Abraham was waiting for the city that has real foundations—the city planned and built by God.

11 He was too old to have children, and Sarah could not have children. It was by faith that Abraham was made able to become a father, because he trusted God to do what he had promised. **12** This man was so old he was almost dead, but from him came as many descendants as there are stars in the sky. Like the sand on the seashore, they could not be counted.

13 All these great people died in faith. They did not get the things that God promised his people, but they saw them coming far in the future and were glad. They said they were like visitors and strangers on earth. **14** When people say such things, they show they are looking for a country that will be their own. **15** If they had been thinking about the country they had left, they could have gone back. **16** But they were waiting for a better country—a heavenly country. So God is not ashamed to be called their God, because he has prepared a city for them.

17 It was by faith that Abraham, when God tested him, offered his son Isaac as a sacrifice. God made the promises to Abraham, but Abraham was ready to offer his own son as a sacrifice. **18** God had said, "The descendants I promised you will be from Isaac." **19** Abraham believed that God could raise the dead, and really, it was as if Abraham got Isaac back from death.

20 It was by faith that Isaac blessed the future of Jacob and Esau. **21** It was by faith that Jacob, as he was dying, blessed each one of Joseph's sons. Then he worshiped as he leaned on the top of his walking stick.

22 It was by faith that Joseph, while he was dying, spoke about the Israelites leaving Egypt and gave instructions about what to do with his body.

23 It was by faith that Moses' parents hid him for three months after he was born. They saw that Moses was a beautiful baby, and they were not afraid to disobey the king's order.

24 It was by faith that Moses, when he grew up, refused to be called the son of the king of Egypt's daughter. **25** He chose to suffer with God's people instead of enjoying sin for a short time. **26** He thought it was better to suffer for the Christ than to have all the treasures of Egypt, because he was looking for God's reward. **27** It was by faith that Moses left Egypt and was not afraid of the king's anger. Moses continued strong as if he could see the God that no one can see. **28** It was by faith that Moses prepared the Passover and spread the blood on the doors so the one who brings death would not kill the firstborn sons of Israel.

29 It was by faith that the people crossed the Red Sea as if it were dry land. But when the Egyptians tried it, they were drowned.

30 It was by faith that the walls of Jericho fell after the people had marched around them for seven days.

31 It was by faith that Rahab, the prostitute, welcomed the spies and was not killed with those who refused to obey God.

32 Do I need to give more examples? I do not have time to tell you about Gideon, Barak, Samson, Jephthah, David, Samuel, and the prophets. **33** Through their faith they defeated kingdoms. They did what was right, received God's promises, and shut the mouths of lions. **24** They stopped great fires and were saved from being killed with swords. They were weak, and yet were made strong. They were powerful in battle and defeated other armies. **35** Women received their dead relatives raised back to life. Others were tortured and refused to accept their freedom so they could be raised from the dead to a better life. **36** Some were laughed at and beaten. Others were put in chains and thrown into prison. **37** They were stoned to death, they were cut in half, and they were killed with swords. Some wore the skins of sheep and goats. They were poor, abused, and treated badly. **38** The world was not good enough for them! They wandered in deserts and mountains, living in caves and holes in the earth.

39 All these people are known for their faith, but none of them received what God had promised. **40** God planned to give us something better so that they would be made perfect, but only together with us.

Hebrews 12:1-2 NKJV – **1** Therefore we also, since we are surrounded by so great a cloud of witnesses, let us lay aside every weight, and the sin which so easily ensnares *us,* and let us run with endurance the race that is set before us, **2** looking unto Jesus, the author and finisher of *our* faith, who for the joy that was set before Him endured the cross, despising the shame, and has sat down at the right hand of the throne of God.

Hebrews 12:22 –But you have come to Mount Zion, to the city of the living God, the heavenly Jerusalem. You have come to thousands of angels gathered together with joy.

Hebrews 13:5-6 – **5** Keep your lives free from the love of money, and be satisfied with what you have. God has said, "I will never leave you; I will never abandon you." *(see Deuteronomy 31:6)*

6 So we can say with confidence, "I will not be afraid, because the Lord is my helper. People can't do anything to me." *(see Psalm 118:6)*

Hebrews 13:20-21 – **20-21** I pray that the God of peace will give you every good thing you need so you can do what he wants. God raised from the dead our Lord Jesus, the Great Shepherd of the sheep, because of the blood of his death. His blood began the eternal agreement that God made with his people. I pray that God will do in us what pleases him, through Jesus Christ, and to him be glory forever and ever. Amen.

JAMES

James 1:2-5 NKJV

Profiting From Trials

2 My brethren, count it all joy when you fall into various trials, **3** knowing that the testing of your faith produces patience. **4** But let patience have *its* perfect work, that you may be perfect and complete, lacking nothing. **5** If any of you lacks wisdom, let him ask of God, who gives to all liberally and without reproach, and it will be given to him.

James 1:12-15

Temptation Is Not from God

12 When people are tempted and still continue strong, they should be happy. After they have proved their faith, God will reward them with life forever. God promised this to all those who love him. **13** When people are tempted, they should not say, "God is tempting me." Evil cannot tempt God, and God himself does not tempt anyone. **14** But people are tempted when their own evil desire leads them away and traps them. **15** This desire leads to sin, and then the sin grows and brings death.

James 1:19-27

Listening and Obeying

19 My dear brothers and sisters, always be willing to listen and slow to speak. Do not become angry easily, **20** because anger will not help you live the right kind of life God wants. **21** So put out of your life every evil thing and every kind of wrong. Then in gentleness accept God's teaching that is planted in your hearts, which can save you.

22 Do what God's teaching says; when you only listen and do nothing, you are fooling yourselves. **23** Those who hear God's teaching and do nothing are like people who look at themselves in a mirror. **24** They see their faces and then go away and quickly forget what they looked like. **25** But the truly happy people are those who carefully study God's perfect law that makes people free, and they continue to study it. They do not forget what they heard, but they obey what God's teaching says. Those who do this will be made happy.

The True Way to Worship God

26 People who think they are religious but say things they should not say are just fooling themselves. Their "religion" is worth nothing. **27** Religion that God the Father accepts as pure and without fault is this: caring for orphans or widows who need help, and keeping yourself free from the world's evil influence.

James 4:8 – Come near to God, and God will come near to you. You sinners, clean sin out of your lives. You who are trying to follow God and the world at the same time, make your thinking pure.
James 4:17 – Anyone who knows the right thing to do, but does not do it, is sinning.
James 5:16 – Confess your sins to each other and pray for each other so God can heal you. When a believing person prays, great things happen.

1 PETER

1 Peter 2:1-12

Jesus Is the Living Stone

1 So then, rid yourselves of all evil, all lying, hypocrisy, jealousy, and evil speech. **2** As newborn babies want milk, you should want the pure and simple teaching. By it you can mature in your salvation, **3** because you have already examined and seen how good the Lord is.

4 Come to the Lord Jesus, the "stone" that lives. The people of the world did not want this stone, but he was the stone God chose, and he was precious. **5** You also are like living stones, so let yourselves be used to build a spiritual temple—to be holy priests who offer spiritual sacrifices to God. He will accept those sacrifices through Jesus Christ. **6** The Scripture says: "I will put a stone in the ground in Jerusalem. Everything will be built on this important and precious rock. Anyone who trusts in him will never be disappointed." *(see Isaiah 28:16)*

7 This stone is worth much to you who believe. But to the people who do not believe, "the stone that the builders rejected has become the cornerstone." *(see Psalm 118:22)*

8 Also, he is "a stone that causes people to stumble, a rock that makes them fall." *(see Isaiah 8:14)*

They stumble because they do not obey what God says, which is what God planned to happen to them.

9 But you are a chosen people, royal priests, a holy nation, a people for God's own possession. You were chosen to tell about the wonderful acts of God, who called you out of darkness into his wonderful light. **10** At one time you were not a people, but now you are God's people. In the past you had never received mercy, but now you have received God's mercy.

Live for God

11 Dear friends, you are like foreigners and strangers in this world. I beg you to avoid the evil things your bodies want to do that fight against your soul. **12** People who do not believe are living all around you and might say that you are doing wrong. Live such good lives that they will see the good things you do and will give glory to God on the day when Christ comes again.

1 Peter 2:25 – You were like sheep that wandered away, but now you have come back to the Shepherd and Overseer of your souls.
1 Peter 3:18 – Christ himself suffered for sins once. He was not guilty, but he suffered for those who are guilty to bring you to God. His body was killed, but he was made alive in the spirit.
1 Peter 3:21 NKJV – There is also an antitype which now saves us—baptism (not the removal of the filth of the flesh, but the answer of a good conscience toward God), through the resurrection of Jesus Christ.
1 Peter 5:4 – Then when Christ, the Chief Shepherd, comes, you will get a glorious crown that will never lose its beauty.
1 Peter 5:8-11 – **8** Control yourselves and be careful! The devil, your enemy, goes around like a roaring lion looking for someone to eat. **9** Refuse to give in to him, by standing strong in your faith. You know that your Christian family all over the world is having the same kinds of suffering.
10 And after you suffer for a short time, God, who gives all grace, will make everything right. He will make you strong and support you and keep you from falling. He called you to share in his glory in Christ, a glory that will continue forever. **11** All power is his forever and ever. Amen.

2 PETER

2 Peter 3:9 NKJV – The Lord is not slack concerning *His* promise, as some count slackness, but is longsuffering toward us, not willing that any should perish but that all should come to repentance.

1 JOHN

1 John 1

The Word of Life

1 We write you now about what has always existed, which we have heard, we have seen with our own eyes, we have looked at, and we have touched with our hands. We write to you about the Word that gives life. **2** He who gives life was shown to us. We saw him and can give proof about it. And now we announce to you that he has life that continues forever. He was with God the Father and was shown to us. **3** We announce to you what we have seen and heard, because we want you also to have fellowship with us. Our fellowship is with God the Father and with his Son, Jesus Christ. **4** We write this to you so we may be full of joy.

Walking in the Light

5 Here is the message we have heard from Christ and now announce to you: God is light, and in him there is no darkness at all. **6** So if we say we have fellowship with God, but we continue living in darkness, we are liars and do not follow the truth. **7** But if we live in the light, as God is in the light, we can share fellowship with each other. Then the blood of Jesus, God's Son, cleanses us from every sin.

8 If we say we have no sin, we are fooling ourselves, and the truth is not in us. **9** But if we confess our sins, he will forgive our sins, because we can trust God to do what is right. He will cleanse us from all the wrongs we have done. **10** If we say we have not sinned, we make God a liar, and we do not accept God's teaching.

1 John 3:1-10

We Are God's Children

1 The Father has loved us so much that we are called children of God. And we really are his children. The reason the people in the world do not know us is that they have not known him. **2** Dear friends, now we are children of God, and we have not yet been shown what we will be in the future. But we know that when Christ comes again, we will be like him, because we will see him as he really is. **3** Christ is pure, and all who have this hope in Christ keep themselves pure like Christ.

4 The person who sins breaks God's law. Yes, sin is living against God's law. **5** You know that Christ came to take away sins and that there is no sin in Christ. **6** So anyone who lives in Christ does not go on sinning. Anyone who goes on sinning has never really understood Christ and has never known him.

7 Dear children, do not let anyone lead you the wrong way. Christ is righteous. So to be like Christ a person must do what is right. **8** The devil has been sinning since the beginning, so anyone who continues to sin belongs to the devil. The Son of God came for this purpose: to destroy the devil's work.

9 Those who are God's children do not continue sinning, because the new life from God remains in them. They are not able to go on sinning, because they have become children of God. **10** So we can see who God's children are and who the devil's children are: Those who do not do what is right are not God's children, and those who do not love their brothers and sisters are not God's children.

1 John 3:14 – We know we have left death and have come into life because we love each other. Whoever does not love is still dead.

1 John 3:22 KJV – And whatsoever we ask, we receive of him, because we keep his commandments, and do those things that are pleasing in his sight.

1 John 4:9-10 – **9** This is how God showed his love to us: He sent his one and only Son into the world so that we could have life through him. **10** This is what real love is: It is not our love for God; it is God's love for us. He sent his Son to die in our place to take away our sins.

1 John 4:19-21 NIV – **19** We love because he first loved us. **20** If anyone says, "I love God," yet hates his brother, he is a liar. For anyone who does not love his brother, whom he has seen, cannot love God, whom he has not seen. **21** And he has given us this command: Whoever loves God must also love his brother.

1 John 5

Faith in the Son of God

1 Everyone who believes that Jesus is the Christ is God's child, and whoever loves the Father also loves the Father's children. **2** This is how we know we love God's children: when we love God and obey his commands. **3** Loving God means obeying his commands. And God's commands are not too hard for us, **4** because everyone who is a child of God conquers the world. And this is the victory that conquers the world—our faith. **5** So the one who conquers the world is the person who believes that Jesus is the Son of God.

6 Jesus Christ is the One who came by water and blood. He did not come by water only, but by water and blood. And the Spirit says that this is true, because the Spirit is the truth. **7** So there are three witnesses: **8** the Spirit, the water, and the blood; and these three witnesses agree. **9** We believe people when they say something is true. But what God says is more important, and he has told us the truth about his own Son. **10** Anyone who believes in the Son of God has the truth that God told us. Anyone who does not believe makes God a liar, because that person does not believe what God told us about his Son. **11** This is what God told us: God has given us eternal life, and this life is in his Son. **12** Whoever has the Son has life, but whoever does not have the Son of God does not have life.

We Have Eternal Life Now

13 I write this letter to you who believe in the Son of God so you will know you have eternal life. **14** And this is the boldness we have in God's presence: that if we ask God for anything that agrees with what he wants, he hears us. **15** If we know he hears us every time we ask him, we know we have what we ask from him.

16 If anyone sees a brother or sister sinning (sin that does not lead to eternal death), that person should pray, and God will give the sinner life. I am talking about people whose sin does not lead to eternal death. There is sin that leads to death. I do not mean that a person should pray about that sin. **17** Doing wrong is always sin, but there is sin that does not lead to eternal death.

18 We know that those who are God's children do not continue to sin. The Son of God keeps them safe, and the Evil One cannot touch them. **19** We know that we belong to God, but the Evil One controls the whole world. **20** We also know that the Son of God has come and has given us understanding so that we can know the True One. And our lives are in the True One and in his Son, Jesus Christ. He is the true God and the eternal life.

21 So, dear children, keep yourselves away from false gods.

REVELATION

Revelation 1:5 – And from Jesus Christ. Jesus is the faithful witness, the first among those raised from the dead. He is the ruler of the kings of the earth. He is the One who loves us, who made us free from our sins with the blood of his death.

Revelation 1:8 – The Lord God says, "I am the Alpha and the Omega. I am the One who is and was and is coming. I am the Almighty."

Revelation 1:18 – I am the One who lives; I was dead, but look, I am alive forever and ever! And I hold the keys to death and to the place of the dead.

Revelation 2

To the Church in Ephesus

1 "Write this to the angel of the church in Ephesus:

"The One who holds the seven stars in his right hand and walks among the seven golden lampstands says this: **2** I know what you do, how you work hard and never give up. I know you do not put up with the false teachings of evil people. You have tested those who say they are apostles but really are not, and you found they are liars. **3** You have patience and have suffered troubles for my name and have not given up.

4 "But I have this against you: You have left the love you had in the beginning. **5** So remember where you were before you fell. Change your hearts and do what you did at first. If you do not change, I will come to you and will take away your lampstand from its place. **6** But there is something you do that is right: You hate what the Nicolaitans do, as much as I.

7 "Every person who has ears should listen to what the Spirit says to the churches. To those who win the victory I will give the right to eat the fruit from the tree of life, which is in the garden of God.

To the Church in Smyrna

8 "Write this to the angel of the church in Smyrna:

"The One who is the First and the Last, who died and came to life again, says this: **9** I know your troubles and that you are poor, but really you are rich! I know the bad things some people say about you. They say they are Jews, but they are not true Jews. They are a synagogue that belongs to Satan. **10** Do not be afraid of what you are about to suffer. I tell you, the devil will put some of you in prison to test you, and you will suffer for ten days. But be faithful, even if you have to die, and I will give you the crown of life.

11 "Everyone who has ears should listen to what the Spirit says to the churches. Those who win the victory will not be hurt by the second death.

To the Church in Pergamum

12 "Write this to the angel of the church in Pergamum:

"The One who has the sharp, double-edged sword says this: **13** I know where you live. It is where Satan has his throne. But you are true to me. You did not refuse to tell about your faith in me even during the time of Antipas, my faithful witness who was killed in your city, where Satan lives.

14 "But I have a few things against you: You have some there who follow the teaching of Balaam. He taught Balak how to cause the people of Israel to sin by eating food offered to idols and by taking part in sexual sins. **15** You also have some who follow the teaching of the Nicolaitans. **16** So change your hearts and lives. If you do not, I will come to you quickly and fight against them with the sword that comes out of my mouth.

17 "Everyone who has ears should listen to what the Spirit says to the churches.

"I will give some of the hidden manna to everyone who wins the victory. I will also give to each one who wins the victory a white stone with a new name written on it. No one knows this new name except the one who receives it.

To the Church in Thyatira

18 "Write this to the angel of the church in Thyatira:

"The Son of God, who has eyes that blaze like fire and feet like shining bronze, says this: **19** I know what you do. I know about your love, your faith, your service, and your patience. I know that you are doing more now than you did at first.

20 "But I have this against you: You let that woman Jezebel spread false teachings. She says she is a prophetess, but by her teaching she leads my people to take part in sexual sins and to eat food that is offered to idols. **21** I have given her time to change her heart and turn away from her sin, but she does not want to change. **22** So I will throw her on a bed of suffering. And all those who take part in adultery with her will suffer greatly if they do not turn away from the wrongs she does. **23** I will also kill her followers. Then all the churches will know I am the One who searches hearts and minds, and I will repay each of you for what you have done.

24 "But others of you in Thyatira have not followed her teaching and have not learned what some call Satan's deep secrets. I say to you that I will not put any other load on you. **25** Only continue in your loyalty until I come.

26 "I will give power over the nations to everyone who wins the victory and continues to be obedient to me until the end. '**27** You will rule over them with an iron rod, as when pottery is broken into pieces.' *(see Psalm 2:9)*

28 This is the same power I received from my Father. I will also give him the morning star. **29** Everyone who has ears should listen to what the Spirit says to the churches.

Revelation 3

To the Church in Sardis

1 "Write this to the angel of the church in Sardis:

"The One who has the seven spirits and the seven stars says this: I know what you do. People say that you are alive, but really you are dead. **2** Wake up! Strengthen what you have left before it dies completely. I have found that what you are doing is less than what my God wants. **3** So do not forget what you have received and heard. Obey it, and change your hearts and lives. So you must wake up, or I will come like a thief, and you will not know when I will come to you. **4** But you have a few there in Sardis who have kept their clothes unstained, so they will walk with me and will wear white clothes, because they are worthy. **5** Those who win the victory will be dressed in white clothes like them. And I will not erase their names from the book of life, but I will say they belong to me before my Father and before his angels. **6** Everyone who has ears should listen to what the Spirit says to the churches.

To the Church in Philadelphia

7 "Write this to the angel of the church in Philadelphia:

"This is what the One who is holy and true, who holds the key of David, says. When he opens a door, no one can close it. And when he closes it, no one can open it. **8** I know what you do. I have put an open door before you, which no one can close. I know you have little strength, but you have obeyed my teaching and were not afraid to speak my name. **9** Those in the synagogue that belongs to Satan say they are Jews, but they are not true Jews; they are liars. I will make them come before you and bow at your feet, and they will know that I have loved you. **10** You have obeyed my teaching about not giving up your faith. So I will keep you from the time of trouble that will come to the whole world to test those who live on earth.

11 "I am coming soon. Continue strong in your faith so no one will take away your crown. **12** I will make those who win the victory pillars in the temple of my God, and they will never have to leave it. I will write on them the name of my God and the name of the city of my God, the new Jerusalem, that comes down out of heaven from my God. I will also write on them my new name. **13** Everyone who has ears should listen to what the Spirit says to the churches.

To the Church in Laodicea

14 "Write this to the angel of the church in Laodicea:

"The Amen, the faithful and true witness, the ruler of all God has made, says this: **15** I know what you do, that you are not hot or cold. I wish that you were hot or cold! **16** But because you are lukewarm—neither hot, nor cold—I am ready to spit you out of my mouth. **17** You say, 'I am rich, and I have become wealthy and do not need anything.' But you do not know that you are really miserable, pitiful, poor, blind, and naked. **18** I advise you to buy from me gold made pure in fire so you can be truly rich. Buy from me white clothes so you can be clothed and so you can cover your shameful nakedness. Buy from me medicine to put on your eyes so you can truly see.

19 "I correct and punish those whom I love. So be eager to do right, and change your hearts and lives. **20** Here I am! I stand at the door and knock. If you hear my voice and open the door, I will come in and eat with you, and you will eat with me.

21 "Those who win the victory will sit with me on my throne in the same way that I won the victory and sat down with my Father on his throne. **22** Everyone who has ears should listen to what the Spirit says to the churches."

Revelation 4:11 – "You are worthy, our Lord and God, to receive glory and honor and power, because you made all things. Everything existed and was made, because you wanted it."

Revelation 5:1-14 NKJV

The Lamb Takes the Scroll

1 And I saw in the right *hand* of Him who sat on the throne a scroll written inside and on the back, sealed with seven seals. **2** Then I saw a strong angel proclaiming with a loud voice, "Who is worthy to open the scroll and to loose its seals?" **3** And no one in heaven or on the earth or under the earth was able to open the scroll, or to look at it.

4 So I wept much, because no one was found worthy to open and read the scroll, or to look at it. **5** But one of the elders said to me, "Do not weep. Behold, the Lion of the tribe of Judah, the Root of David, has prevailed to open the scroll and to loose its seven seals."

6 And I looked, and behold, in the midst of the throne and of the four living creatures, and in the midst of the elders, stood a Lamb as though it had been slain, having seven horns and seven eyes, which are the seven Spirits of God sent out into all the earth. **7** Then He came and took the scroll out of the right hand of Him who sat on the throne.

Worthy Is the Lamb

8 Now when He had taken the scroll, the four living creatures and the twenty-four elders fell down before the Lamb, each having a harp, and golden bowls full of incense, which are the prayers of the saints. **9** And they sang a new song, saying: You are worthy to take the scroll, And to open its seals; for You were slain, and have redeemed us to God by Your blood out of every tribe and tongue and people and nation, **10** And have made us kings and priests to our God; And we shall reign on the earth."

11 Then I looked, and I heard the voice of many angels around the throne, the living creatures, and the elders; and the number of them was ten thousand times ten thousand, and thousands of thousands, **12** saying with a loud voice: "Worthy is the Lamb who was slain to receive power and riches and wisdom, and strength and honor and glory and blessing!"

13 And every creature which is in heaven and on the earth and under the earth and such as are in the sea, and all that are in them, I heard saying: "Blessing and honor and glory and power be to Him who sits on the throne, and to the Lamb, forever and ever!"

14 Then the four living creatures said, "Amen!" And the twenty-four elders fell down and worshiped Him who lives forever and ever.

Revelation 7:9-10 NKJV – **9** After these things I looked, and behold, a great multitude which no one could number, of all nations, tribes, peoples, and tongues, standing before the throne and before the Lamb, clothed with white robes, with palm branches in their hands, **10** and crying out with a loud voice, saying, "Salvation *belongs* to our God who sits on the throne, and to the Lamb!"

Revelation 7:16-17 – **16** Those people will never be hungry again, and they will never be thirsty again. The sun will not hurt them, and no heat will burn them, **17** because the Lamb at the center of the throne will be their shepherd. He will lead them to springs of water that give life. And God will wipe away every tear from their eyes."

Revelation 11:15-18 NKJV – **15** Then the seventh angel sounded: And there were loud voices in heaven, saying, "The kingdoms of this world have become *the kingdoms* of our Lord and of His Christ, and He shall reign forever and ever!" **16** And the twenty-four elders who sat before God on their thrones fell on their faces and worshiped God, **17** saying: "We give You thanks, O Lord God Almighty, the One who is and who was and who is to come because You have taken Your great power and reigned. **18** The nations were angry, and Your wrath has come, and the time of the dead, that they should be judged, and that You should reward Your servants the prophets and the saints, and those who fear Your name, small and great, and should destroy those who destroy the earth."

Revelation 12:10-11 – **10** Then I heard a loud voice in heaven saying: "The salvation and the power and the kingdom of our God and the authority of his Christ have now come. The accuser of our brothers and sisters, who accused them day and night before our God, has been thrown down. **11** And our brothers and sisters defeated him by the blood of the Lamb's death and by the message they preached. They did not love their lives so much that they were afraid of death.

Revelation 12:17 – Then the dragon was very angry at the woman, and he went off to make war against all her other children—those who obey God's commands and who have the message Jesus taught.

Revelation 14:4-7 – **4** These are the ones who were not defiled with women, for they are virgins. These are the ones who follow the Lamb wherever He goes. These were redeemed from *among* men, *being* firstfruits to God and to the Lamb. **5** And in their mouth was found no deceit, for they are without fault before the throne of God. **6** Then I saw another angel flying high in the air. He had the eternal Good News to preach to those who live on earth—to every nation, tribe, language, and people. **7** He preached in a loud voice, "Fear God and give him praise, because the time has come for God to judge all people. So worship God who made the heavens, and the earth, and the sea, and the springs of water."

Revelation 19:11-16 NKJV – **11** Now I saw heaven opened, and behold, a white horse. And He who sat on him *was* called Faithful and True, and in righteousness He judges and makes war. **12** His eyes *were* like a flame of fire, and on His head *were* many crowns. He had a name written that no one knew except Himself. **13** He *was* clothed with a robe dipped in blood, and His name is called The Word of God. **14** And the armies in heaven, clothed in fine linen, white and clean followed Him on white horses. **15** Now out of His mouth goes a sharp sword, that with it He should strike the nations. And He Himself will rule them with a rod of iron. He Himself treads the winepress of the fierceness and wrath of Almighty God. **16** And He has on *His* robe and on His thigh a name written: KING OF KINGS AND LORD OF LORDS.

Revelation 20:12 NIV – And I saw the dead, great and small, standing before the throne, and books were opened. Another book was opened, which is the book of life. The dead were judged according to what they had done as recorded in the books.

Revelation 20:15 NKJV – And anyone not found written in the Book of Life was cast into the lake of fire.

Revelation 21

The New Jerusalem

1 Then I saw a new heaven and a new earth. The first heaven and the first earth had disappeared, and there was no sea anymore. **2** And I saw the holy city, the new Jerusalem, coming down out of heaven from God. It was prepared like a bride dressed for her husband. **3** And I heard a loud voice from the throne, saying, "Now God's presence is with people, and he will live with them, and they will be his people. God himself will be with them and will be their God. **4** He will wipe away every tear from their eyes, and there will be no more death, sadness, crying, or pain, because all the old ways are gone."

5 The One who was sitting on the throne said, "Look! I am making everything new!" Then he said, "Write this, because these words are true and can be trusted."

6 The One on the throne said to me, "It is finished. I am the Alpha and the Omega, the Beginning and the End. I will give free water from the spring of the water of life to anyone who is thirsty. **7** Those who win the victory will receive this, and I will be their God, and they will be my children. **8** But cowards, those who refuse to believe, who do evil things, who kill, who sin sexually, who do evil magic, who worship idols, and who tell lies—all these will have a place in the lake of burning sulfur. This is the second death."

9 Then one of the seven angels who had the seven bowls full of the seven last troubles came to me, saying, "Come with me, and I will show you the bride, the wife of the Lamb." **10** And the angel carried me away by the Spirit to a very large and high mountain. He showed me the holy city, Jerusalem, coming down out of heaven from God. **11** It was shining with the glory of God and was bright like a very expensive jewel, like a jasper, clear as crystal. **12** The city had a great high wall with twelve gates with twelve angels at the gates, and on each gate was written the name of one of the twelve tribes of Israel. **13** There were three gates on the east, three on the north, three on the south, and three on the west. **14** The walls of the city were built on twelve foundation stones, and on the stones were written the names of the twelve apostles of the Lamb.

15 The angel who talked with me had a measuring rod made of gold to measure the city, its gates, and its wall. **16** The city was built in a square, and its length was equal to its width. The angel measured the city with the rod. The city was 1,500 miles long, 1,500 miles wide, and 1,500 miles high. **17** The angel also measured the wall. It was 216 feet high, by human measurements, which the angel was using. **18** The wall was made of jasper, and the city was made of pure gold, as pure as glass. **19** The foundation stones of the city walls were decorated with every kind of jewel. The first foundation was jasper, the second was sapphire, the third was chalcedony, the fourth was emerald, **20** the fifth was onyx, the sixth was carnelian, the seventh was chrysolite, the eighth was beryl, the ninth was topaz, the tenth was chrysoprase, the eleventh was jacinth, and the twelfth was amethyst. **21** The twelve gates were twelve pearls, each gate having been made from a single pearl. And the street of the city was made of pure gold as clear as glass.

22 I did not see a temple in the city, because the Lord God Almighty and the Lamb are the city's temple. **23** The city does not need the sun or the moon to shine on it, because the glory of God is its light, and the Lamb is the city's lamp. **24** By its light the people of the world will walk, and the kings of the earth will bring their glory into it. **25** The city's gates will never be shut on any day, because there is no night there. **26** The glory and the honor of the nations will be brought into it. **27** Nothing unclean and no one who does shameful things or tells lies will ever go into it. Only those whose names are written in the Lamb's book of life will enter the city.

Revelation 22:1-7

The River of Life

1 Then the angel showed me the river of the water of life. It was shining like crystal and was flowing from the throne of God and of the Lamb **2** down the middle of the street of the city. The tree of life was on each side of the river. It produces fruit twelve times a year, once each month. The leaves of the tree are for the healing of all the nations. **3** Nothing that God judges guilty will be in that city. The throne of God and of the Lamb will be there, and God's servants will worship him. **4** They will see his face, and his name will be written on their foreheads. **5** There will never be night again. They will not need the light of a lamp or the light of the sun, because the Lord God will give them light. And they will rule as kings forever and ever.

6 The angel said to me, "These words can be trusted and are true." The Lord, the God of the spirits of the prophets, sent his angel to show his servants the things that must happen soon.

Jesus Is Coming

7 "Listen! I am coming soon! Blessed is the one who obeys the words of prophecy in this book."

Revelation 22:17 – The Spirit and the bride say, "Come!" Let the one who hears this say, "Come!" Let whoever is thirsty come; whoever wishes may have the water of life as a free gift.

Revelation 22:20 – Jesus, the One who says these things are true, says, "Yes, I am coming soon." Amen. Come, Lord Jesus!

Jesus Prays for Himself

1 Jesus spoke these words, lifted up His eyes to heaven, and said: "Father, the hour has come. Glorify Your Son, that Your Son also may glorify You, 2 as You have given Him authority over all flesh, that He should give eternal life to as many as You have given Him. 3 And this is eternal life, that they may know You, the only true God, and Jesus Christ whom You have sent. 4 I have glorified You on the earth. I have finished the work which You have given Me to do. 5 And now, O Father, glorify Me together with Yourself, with the glory which I had with You before the world was.

Jesus Prays for His Disciples

6 "I have manifested Your name to the men whom You have given Me out of the world. They were Yours, You gave them to Me, and they have kept Your word. 7 Now they have known that all things which You have given Me are from You. 8 For I have given to them the words which You have given Me; and they have received them, and have known surely that I came forth from You; and they have believed that You sent Me.

9 "I pray for them. I do not pray for the world but for those whom You have given Me, for they are Yours. 10 And all Mine are Yours, and Yours are Mine, and I am glorified in them. 11 Now I am no longer in the world, but these are in the world, and I come to You. Holy Father, keep through Your name those whom You have given Me, that they may be one as We are. 12 While I was with them in the world, I kept them in Your name. Those whom You gave Me I have kept; and none of them is lost except the son of perdition, that the Scripture might be fulfilled. 13 But now I come to You, and these things I speak in the world, that they may have My joy fulfilled in themselves. 14 I have given them Your word; and the world has hated them because they are not of the world, just as I am not of the world. 15 I do not pray that You should take them out of the world, but that You should keep them from the evil one. 16 They are not of the world, just as I am not of the world. 17 Sanctify them by Your truth. Your word is truth. 18 As You sent Me into the world, I also have sent them into the world. 19 And for their sakes I sanctify Myself, that they also may be sanctified by the truth.

Jesus Prays for All Believers

20 "I do not pray for these alone, but also for those who will believe in Me through their word; 21 that they all may be one, as You, Father, are in Me, and I in You; that they also may be one in Us, that the world may believe that You sent Me. 22 And the glory which You gave Me I have given them, that they may be one just as We are one: 23 I in them, and You in Me; that they may be made perfect in one, and that the world may know that You have sent Me, and have loved them as You have loved Me.

24 "Father, I desire that they also whom You gave Me may be with Me where I am, that they may behold My glory which You have given Me; for You loved Me before the foundation of the world. 25 O righteous Father! The world has not known You, but I have known You; and these have known that You sent Me. 26 And I have declared to them Your name, and will declare it, that the love with which You loved Me may be in them, and I in them."

(John 17:1-26 NKJV)

Thank You, Father, for Your amazing Word out of Your ancient, holy book. How vividly it brings to our minds history's greatest prayer – The Lord's Prayer *(Matthew 6:9-13 KJV)* – and the assurance that, You, the God of history is still moving in the affairs of mankind, controlling events just as You predicted You

would. With the first coming of Christ, Your Son, the Old Covenant is fulfilled *(Genesis 3:15; Hebrews 8:6-8 NLT; Exodus 20:1-17 NIV)*, and the New Covenant *(Matthew 22:36-40 NLT)* through Him has come as You promised in Your plan of Salvation to establish Your Kingdom on earth, then Christ will come back to rule, and we shall never be separated from You again. You are a God who never withdraws Your promises. Your saving actions in human life and the story of our Salvation, gives true meaning to Your message that we were created for a purpose by an all-loving God who actively participates in all human life, and wants us to live with Him ... forever!

NOTES

⌒

1. Host Webpage: www.christianarticons.com; Image Name: **Jesus**.JP1; Details: 100 x 150 pixels – 7.7kB.

2. **Chapter One**
   Host Webpage: www.whatsaiththescripture.com/WStS.
   Jehovah.html; Image Name: my.LORD.Jesus.JPG;
   Details: 287 x 421 pixels – 9.9kB.

3. **Chapter Two**
   Host Webpage: http://www.ourchurch.com/member/
   n/newjoyministry; Image Name: 1jesusprayed1.JPG;
   Details: 204 x 272 pixels – 9.6kB – JPEG.

4. Special Note: It is not our intention to impose a personality upon God nor form an imagery of the deity of God. By no means are any images included in this manuscript meant to accurately portray the appearance of God or to limit Him in anyway. At best, images are more the creation of the artist's subjective experience than a reflection of God's likeness and personality. These images are not meant to be worshipped or used in the practice of worship. They merely stand as visual representations.

5. All writings in this manuscript are subordinated to the interpretation of Scripture.